DATE DUE			

The Editor

ELY CHINOY is Mary Huggins Gamble Professor of Sociology at Smith College, where he has been a member of the faculty since 1951. He received his B.A. from the University of Newark (now the Newark Colleges of Rutgers University) and his Ph.D. from Columbia University. Prior to coming to Smith he taught at the Newark College of Engineering, New York University, and the University of Toronto. He has been a Fulbright Professor at the University of Leicester in England and in the Philippines and has also taught at Clark University, Mt. Holyoke College, and Amherst College. He is the author of *Automobile Workers and the American Dream, Sociological Perspective, Society: An Introduction to Sociology,* and articles in several books and various scholarly journals.

THE URBAN

EDITED BY

FUTURE

Ely Chinoy

L

LIEBER-ATHERTON

New York 1973

The Urban Future
edited by Ely Chinoy

Address all inquiries to:
Lieber-Atherton, Incorporated
1841 Broadway
New York, New York 10023

Library of Congress Catalog Number 70–169502
ISBN 0-88311-200-0 (cloth); 0-88311-201-9 (paper)

Printed in the United States of America

Contents

THE URBAN FUTURE

Introduction: Trends and Prospects

ELY CHINOY

As our attention has been increasingly and belatedly directed toward the problems of our cities, it has become more and more apparent that the city can no longer be thought of or dealt with by itself, and apart from the rest of American society. The problems that constitute the contemporary "urban crisis"—slums and housing, physical deterioration, crime, underfinanced local governments and overtaxed property owners, inadequate public services, deficient educational facilities and programs, racial conflict, poverty and overburdened welfare rolls, congested traffic and inadequate mass transportation, pollution of air and water—are not confined to the cities, even though their most acute manifestations are often found there.

Sociologists have conventionally distinguished sharply between the urban and the nonurban, between the city and the small town or rural countryside. They emphasized the size, density, and heterogeneity of the city and its distinctive values, life styles, forms of social organization, patterns of social interaction, and economic activities. But as cities have grown and urban populations have spread, these distinctions between the urban and the nonurban have become blurred. Increasingly elaborate networks of transportation and communication have diffused urban culture so widely that traditional contrasts have been substantially diminished. City, suburb, town, and countryside have been progressively integrated into larger and more encompassing social, economic, and political structures.

Like the sociologists, political scientists, and economists, urban planners are finding their conventional perspectives increasingly inadequate as guides to the contemporary urban scene. Students of urban government and politics are largely agreed that present legal boundaries rarely define areas that make political or administrative sense, though there is no consensus as to the merits of either greater neighborhood control of some local functions, or of various forms of metropolitan or regional government. Economists, who may see the city as a locational matrix for economic activity or as an economic unit to be analyzed in terms of inputs and outputs, find that noneconomic factors and external economic circumstances affect, or even determine, the city's economic life. The economic problems located within the city frequently turn out to require action on a larger stage—the region, the state, the nation. Urban planners, too, often discover that their efforts to solve the city's problems cannot be confined within its boundaries and are therefore led to larger considerations and wider perspectives.

If traditional definitions of the city—sociological, economic, political—are no longer adequate, what alternative perspectives can be brought to bear? In view of the changes that have taken place, or are taking place, what are the relevant contexts for the analysis of urban problems? Should attention be focused upon the metropolitan area, the region, or, where it exists, the megalopolis? Would it be enough merely to distinguish between city and suburb, the metropolitan center and the "ring" that surrounds it, and to explore the relations between them? Or does the changing shape and structure of urban America require totally new ways of thinking about the urban community?

There are, of course, no ready answers to these questions. The conventional sociological analysis may continue to have validity for part of the urban world, even as new and different urban forms appear. With increasing scale and complexity, the focus of attention may have to be the relationships among the various forms of urban development—neighborhood, central city, suburb, satellite city, metropolitan region, megalopolis. As John Friedmann and John Miller assert, perhaps the city can no longer be seen as "a physical entity," but must be viewed as "a pattern of point locations and connecting flows of people, information, money, and commodities."[1] Moreover, the urban future is so uncertain and problematic that what seems to make theoretical sense today may be wrong or inadequate tomorrow. As David Riesman once remarked: "Events continually outdistance our attempts to understand them; social scientists, no less than other people, must structure the world while at the same time keeping up with it."[2]

Rather than "try to freeze some knife-edge moment," in C. Wright Mills's graphic phrase, it may be more fruitful to examine the direction in which urban society is moving. Whatever urban America is like today, it is sure to be somewhat different tomorrow. Perhaps by examining what the future may hold in store we can more readily understand the present, cope with its problems, and deliberately and consciously contribute to the shape of the future.

Prediction is an uncertain enterprise deemed appropriate for soothsayers, prophets, and visionaries, but usually avoided by social scientists. Often oriented more to the past than to the future, concerned with facts rather than speculation, sensitive to the complexity of social structure and historical processes, and keenly aware of the still rudimentary level of many of their theories, social scientists characteristically limit themselves to short-run, carefully hedged predictions—if they venture even that far. Few sociologists have tried to see what urban America may become, though their failure to do so inevitably limits their ability to serve the function they claim for themselves—enabling men to help shape their own future.* Unless men can to some degree anticipate the alternatives open to them they will necessarily remain captive to forces which they do not understand and over which they have no control.

To explore the future—or possible futures—does not require, as some might fear, a commitment to a rigid determinism or a venture into uncertain prophecy. It entails instead consideration of present trends and of the social and cultural variables that may affect them, analysis of urban problems and possible solutions, and a careful review of the proposals of planners, politicians, and even visionaries for remaking our cities and for controlling or directing anticipated growth.

The basic urban trends that have emerged during the past several decades can be summarized as follows:

(1) Metropolitan areas have grown more rapidly than other parts of the nation and an increasing proportion of the total population is found in them. Between 1950 and 1960, the 212 Standard Metropolitan Statistical Areas identified in the 1960 Census grew by 26.4 per cent, compared with a national increase of only 18.5 per cent. During that decade, 87 per cent of the total population growth was concentrated in these metropolitan areas. Between 1960 and 1969, the national population grew by 12.2 per cent and the SMSAs by 14.4 per cent; in 1969, 64.5 per cent of all Americans resided in metropolitan areas, and in 1968, only 56.8 per cent lived in the 100 largest areas.[3]

(2) The growth of metropolitan areas, like that of the population as a whole, has been greater in some parts of the country than in others. Of the 24 SMSAs that increased by at least 50 per cent between 1950 and 1960, all but one were in the South

* "Futurology" or "futurism," which has received a good deal of attention recently, has drawn upon many disciplines, but it still involves relatively few scholars and has not significantly affected the dominant perspectives in contemporary social science.

or the West; six were in California, six in Florida, and three in Texas. Of the six that more than doubled during that decade, two were in Florida, two in Texas, one in California, and one in Arizona. Between 1960 and 1965, 35 SMSAs grew by 15 per cent or more; all but five were in the South or the West. Ten areas increased by 25 per cent or more; of these, five were in California, two in Nevada, and the remaining three in the south. Of the 100 largest SMSAs in 1968, ten had grown by 25 per cent or more since 1960; nine of these were in the South or the West, the sole exception being the Washington area.[4]

(3) Within the metropolitan areas, the central cities have been growing more slowly than the suburbs, in some cases even losing population. Between 1940 and 1950 the metropolitan population outside the central cities increased by just over one-third, the cities themselves by only 13.9 per cent. Comparable figures for the 1950s were 48.5 per cent and 10.8 per cent. In 46 SMSAs, chiefly in the northeast, the central cities reported fewer residents. Though the national rate of population growth slowed during the 1960s, the suburban areas continued to increase more rapidly than the cities, growing by 28.2 per cent while the total central city population showed an increase of only 1.3 per cent.

(4) Within many of the central cities there has been a significant and widely noted change in the composition of the population. Large numbers of whites have moved out and large numbers of blacks have moved in. Between 1960 and 1969, more than two million whites left the central cities while 3.5 million blacks were added to their population. By 1969, 55 per cent of all blacks lived in metropolitan centers, and 21 per cent of the central city population was black, with higher concentrations in the larger cities. In 1966, the twelve largest metropolitan centers contained one-third of the entire black population. These racial changes were linked with changes in class composition, for many of the whites who moved out were in the middle class, and most of the blacks who moved in, particularly those from the rural south, had limited education and few occupational skills. In suburban areas the proportion of blacks has remained relatively low

(less than 5 per cent) for at least two decades despite the extensive suburban growth and the massive black migration.

(5) The physical form of cities has also been changing, particularly those whose major growth followed World War II. Usually dependent upon the automobile rather than mass transportation, they resemble suburbs much more than traditional cities. They are much more dispersed, have not developed concentrated central business districts (relying instead upon neighborhood shopping centers), and have not reached population densities comparable to those of older cities. Cleveland, Chicago, and Detroit, all of which lost population between 1950 and 1960, still had population densities of roughly 10,800, 10,000, and 15,800 per square mile, compared with densities of 2,800 in Houston (which almost tripled between 1940 and 1960) and 5,500 in Los Angeles (which increased by 28 per cent between 1950 and 1960 and by almost 65 per cent between 1940 and 1960).

(6) Metropolitan growth outside the central cities has, on the whole, been unplanned and uncontrolled. In some areas this growth has taken place gradually and often casually, as homes, shops, gasoline stations, drive-in movies, restaurants, shopping centers, factories, and offices have been located wherever individuals (or corporations) found it convenient or desirable. In other places it has come all at once as developers built whole communities, sometimes in the form of housing projects lacking any provision for community needs, elsewhere with carefully planned inclusion of needed utilities and educational, religious, recreational, and shopping facilities. The wave of suburban expansion has created new communities of many kinds even as it rolls over and swallows preexisting farm communities, residential suburbs, and satellite cities. Metropolitan areas have become mixtures including the central city, with all its diversity; residential suburbs that vary widely in their class composition; satellite cities, some of which are experiencing the same processes of growth and change as the central cities; distinct commercial and industrial areas; and a rural-urban fringe that can include, often in chaotic fashion, everything—farms, factories, shops, offices,

residences, service facilities, community institutions. In each area, these varied elements are tied together by networks of highways and by mass transportation systems that, if they exist at all, are becoming more and more inadequate and inefficient.

(7) Although the central city continues to provide jobs for many suburban residents, the economic balance seems to be shifting away from the once overwhelming predominance of the city. Not only does the growing suburban population (in 1968 roughly 70,000,000 compared to only 58,000,000 in the central cities) require services and facilities close at hand, but an increasing number of jobs are being created by industries that are located in suburban areas, sometimes starting from scratch, sometimes migrating from the cities. Improved means of transportation and communication and the development of new sources of energy have increasingly made it possible to decentralize many of the activities once thought of as necessarily confined to the city—manufacturing and wholesaling, for example. Those activities that remain in the city—finance, publishing, advertising, mass communication, insurance, business and professional services, and light industry—do so because of the need for face-to-face contact and the "external economies" that physical proximity to diversified economic activities allow.

(8) As some metropolitan areas expanded, they gradually came to form what Jean Gottman has described as "megalopolis," a "cluster of metropolitan areas" that can be considered in some respects as a new urban form. In the northeast, where this development is most advanced, megalopolis extends from north of Boston to northern Virginia and from the Atlantic coast to the foothills of the Appalachians. Comparable developments are taking place in southern California from San Diego to Los Angeles and Santa Barbara; in various parts of the midwest—from Milwaukee to Chicago and northwestern Indiana, for example; and on a much more modest scale along the Gulf Coast in Texas, in the Pacific northwest from Seattle to Portland, and in the area around San Francisco that includes San Jose and Sacramento. There are open areas within the megalopolis that could be de-

fined as rural, but they are in effect part of the complex economic, social, and cultural systems that radiate from the metropolitan centers. Each central city has its own tributary area, though it may have to compete for influence over outlying districts that feel the pull of another metropolitan center, and one of the central cities may predominate; New York, for example, or Los Angeles, or Chicago. Yet the various metropolitan centers are tied together in diverse ways that seem to justify considering the entire area, for some purposes at least, a single entity.[5]

If these trends were to persist, what would urban America be like in the future? The most obvious result would be an increasing division between cities and suburbs. Cities would be the home of the rich and the poor, with a large proportion of the latter made up of blacks and, in the northeast, Puerto Ricans, in the southwest, Mexicans. Concomitantly, many cities would lose population and experience declining densities. Under these circumstances, the cities would continue to deteriorate, their physical plants aging and poorly maintained, public services inadequate to the demands placed upon them, economic life declining, and amenities diminishing.

The suburbs would remain predominantly white (even if there were a modest increase in the number of blacks living there) and middle class, though including some of the rich and many of the better paid blue-collar workers. Suburban densities would probably increase as more people left the cities and more industry was located in outlying areas. One could anticipate that eventually suburbs would face many of the same problems as the cities (as many already do): the disappearance of accessible open space, congested roads, overcrowded facilities, pollution of air and water, and increasing tax costs. The last would lead, and has already in many places, to efforts to attract more business and industry, thus reinforcing the tendencies toward greater concentration in the suburbs.

To extrapolate from the past into the future in this fashion is a risky venture. The underlying conditions that have contributed to past trends may change, and events that cannot be anticipated now may affect the rate of change or shift its direction. Indeed, the analysis of the future may itself influence the form the future takes. Despite these uncertainties and the inevitable historical discontinuities, one can identify some of the variables that will in all likelihood affect future trends and sketch in what seem to be the major alternatives. Indeed, the greater our awareness of the forces at work and of problems and possibilities, the greater the likelihood that public—and private—policies and programs can help to shape a future closer to human wishes and desires.

Of fundamental importance in determining the urban future is the size of the population and the rate of growth. Most population growth will probably take place in metropolitan areas, as it has for the past three decades. A rapid increase in the urban population would place great strain on institutions and facilities that in many areas already find it difficult to satisfy immediate needs. Heavy investment would be required for new homes, schools, hospitals, roads, sewage plants, and other facilities at a time when there are already pressing demands to make up for past deficiencies and to cope with newly recognized problems such as the despoiling of the environment. A lower rate of growth would ease—though certainly not remove—the strains, and might allow for more effective planning and easier solutions to both present problems and those that a substantial growth in metropolitan populations would bring.

The uncertainties of demographic prediction are evident in the various projections prepared by the United States Bureau of the Census during the 1960s.[6] In 1964 the Bureau offered four estimates of the population growth to 1990 that ranged from a low of 256 million to a high of 300 million. (The National Committee on Urban Growth Policy recently predicted that by the year 2000 the urban population alone will have increased by 100 million.)[7] Since the actual increase between 1964 and 1970 has been close to the lowest of the four projections, it seems likely, in view of lowered birth rates and growing concern about the relationship between population growth and the environment, that the population increase during the next two decades will be considerably lower than anticipated. In a detailed analysis of future metropolitan population based upon the second lowest Census Bureau projection of total growth, Patricia Hodge and Philip Hauser estimated in 1968 that by 1985 the metropolitan population will total 178 million.[8] If, however, the total increase were to approximate the lowest Census Bureau projection, the metropolitan population will be only about 167 million in 1985. Even this lowest estimate would entail an increase of approximately 37 million people in need of homes, jobs, schools, recreational facilities, and all the other requisites of existence.

On the basis of past trends, one would expect that whatever the total metropolitan growth, most of it would occur in suburban areas rather than in the central cities. Hodge and Hauser, for example, anticipate that 10 per cent of the total increase from 1960 to 1985 will occur in the central cities while 79 per cent will be absorbed by the suburban rings. In 1985, they estimate, only 37 per cent of the metropolitan population will be living in central cities with 63 per cent in the rings, compared with 52 per cent and 48 per cent respectively in 1960. According to their figures, we may anticipate an increase of just over 7 million in the cities and 58 million in the suburbs.

All of these estimates simply extrapolate from present statistical trends. On what substantive rather than statistical grounds can one justify such metropolitan projections? What circumstances might accelerate or slow down these trends, or even change their direction entirely?

The growth of cities in the United States was closely linked to industrialization and economic expansion—and based upon the increasing efficiency of agriculture. Although cities antedated industrialization, their substantial growth during the nineteenth century was stimulated by the increase in manufacturing and the correlative growth in trade and commerce. Economic opportunities in the city drew migrants. The enlarged scale of industrial and economic organization and the need to be relatively close to the place of employment increased population density as well as numbers.

With improved means of transportation and communication, however, urban populations could disperse. Greater ease of movement increased the range of opportunities open to workers at all levels and enabled them to move further away from their place of employment. They could more readily separate residence and workplace, thus enlarging their choice of jobs, homes, and life styles. Improved transportation and communication also enlarged the tributary areas of the city to which it supplied goods and services and over which it could exert its influence.

There are limits, based on the time and cost of travel, on the extent to which residence and workplace can be separated. Of crucial importance, therefore, in determining the extent of metropolitan dispersion is the distribution of jobs; that is, the location of economic activity. As the trends of recent decades so clearly show, new sources of power and new means of transportation and communication have increasingly freed industry from the confines of the central city. Steam power must be used close to where it is produced. But electrical power can be transmitted economically over large distances, allowing industry to make its locational decisions on other grounds. With the advent of the automobile and truck, industry no longer had to be close to fixed transportation lines—the street car, subway, railroad, waterway—for access to its labor supply, raw materials, and disposal of the finished product. Concomitantly, the telephone diminished the need for face-to-face contact.

As noted earlier, some types of economic enterprise—finance, communication, insurance, small scale light industry—continue to find advantageous or necessary the easy personal access and external economies based on proximity. But even these types of activity are finding the advantages of central location less important than they once were. Clearly, then, in the absence of other reasons for remaining in the central city, economic activity may continue to leave, particularly if the disadvantages of the city—

high taxes and high land costs, limited space for expansion, the general unattractiveness and deterioration of the urban environment—become increasingly acute and apparent. In a recent analysis of the distribution of jobs in metropolitan areas, John Kain concluded that:

> City and suburb are already becoming similar. Over the long haul, these processes could result in a relatively "flat" distribution of employment and population that is sharply different from what we know today and even less like that we remember of the historic city.[9]

What is happening, it would appear, is the attenuation, if not eventual disappearance, of the economic functions once thought of as distinctively urban.

Where people live, however, is only partially dependent upon where the jobs are. It is also affected by the kind of life style they wish to follow. They may be quite willing to accept the economic, physical, psychic, and social costs of a substantial separation of home and workplace in order to live in a particular way. Much of the massive migration to the suburbs during the past twenty-five years has, in fact, stemmed from a desire for the style of life to be found there. Some of those who left the city have probably done so regretfully, pushed out by circumstances over which they felt they had no control, such as increasing noise and dirt, deteriorating public services, and growing dangers to self and property. But by far the greater number have anticipated positive gains that greatly outweighed the advantages, if any, they might have seen in the city.

Although suburbs are not all alike, often differing along class lines, the various studies of suburban communities reveal a set of values, interests, and concerns that constitute a more or less distinctive cultural pattern and life style. Of central importance in this pattern is the desire for a home of one's own and for more space: a larger house, an open lawn or backyard, greater and safer play space for children. Home ownership, a cherished traditional American value, has been much more readily achieved in the suburbs where the free-standing, one-family home at a wide range of prices has been the norm, rather than the multi-family building characteristic of the city. (It should be noted that the post-World War II government programs that encouraged home building in the suburbs and facilitated their sale by easing the problem of financing, were administered in such a way that most Negroes were excluded.)

The desire for more space and for home ownership is part of a set of values that can best be described as familistic.[10] These values center on children (a frequent reason for the move to the suburbs has been the search for better schools and a better environment for growing up), collective family activities, and the acquisition of possessions that are useful not only in maintaining the home but also in marking the family's status in the community. The family, as many observers have noted, has long ceased to be a significant productive unit in the economy; instead, it is now essentially a consuming unit. Major purchases—a home, a car, household appliances—are family decisions rather than individual choices. The suburbanite, of course, has no monopoly on the acquisitiveness of the American consumer, but he has perhaps greater opportunities for the use and display of the seemingly endless fruits of American technology: a second car, power lawn mower, outdoor swimming pool, or home freezer, to mention but a few.

Life in the suburbs is also seen as quieter and more relaxed than life in the city, more casual, and less hurried. Hopefully it can allow "privacy from neighbors and freedom of action and self-expression."[11] The city encourages anonymity, but it does not readily permit escape from the presence of others. It provides a wide range of cultural opportunities, but access to them may be limited because of intense competition for their use. Though there are fewer cultural facilities in the suburb, there are other activities that draw many people—gardening, outdoor sports, hobbies that require more space in the home or outdoors than is usually available in the city.

As is evident in this list of activities, much of the "self-expression" promised by the suburb is to be found in leisure pursuits. Indeed, it is in suburban communities that the pervasive shift from "production values" to those of consumption that has been taking place for many years has probably gone farthest.[12] Suburban life, to be sure, is not reduced simply to leisure, just as urban life is not totally committed to work and success. Men who live in the suburbs must still support their families and their careers remain important, even central, in their lives. Many women find suburban domesticity, leisure, and community life confining, and seek out other activities that satisfy their needs and interests. But in the balancing of work and play, leisure now seems to occupy a more important place in suburban values and the suburban life style than it does in the city. It is at least in part the interest in outdoor leisure activities that accounts for the fact that the most rapidly growing areas in the nation are to be found in the South and the Southwest where the outdoor life can be most easily pursued the year round.

This casual, family-centered, leisure-oriented style of life is most readily pursued in a homogeneous community in which it is relatively easy, if one chooses, to participate socially and politically. Social differences do not totally disappear, but the class composition of many suburbs is limited to a narrow range, ethnic clusters often appear, and Negroes have been virtually excluded. Although the stereotype of the overorganized, oversociable suburb no longer has much currency, the ease with which social relationships can be established and the prevalence and accessability of community organizations are highly valued by some, perhaps many, suburbanites, particularly in the upper-middle class areas.

Many of the values inherent in this suburban way of life are not new. Nor are suburbs, which are to be found, in one form or another, outside cities almost everywhere. But increasing affluence and greater "automobility," together with the geographical dispersion of business and industry, have opened the suburbs to large numbers of people who would not have been able to move there in the past, when only the well-to-do could afford to live outside the city. If these values retain their hold and continue to seem more easily realized in the suburbs than in the city, then one would expect that the drift toward the suburbs will continue.

Despite the pervasiveness of familistic, leisure-oriented values, there are those who continue to prefer a more distinctively urban life style to the prevailing mode of suburban life. Space is less important to them than accessability to the facilities and opportunities they find in the city. Diversity and variety are preferred to homogeneity, the liveliness and excitement of city streets to the casual and relaxed ways of the suburb. Though leisure pursuits may be equally valued, their forms are different —shopping, theatre, and night life, rather than gardening, cook-outs, and outdoor sports. Anonymity and freedom from the restraints of a small community are preferred to the opportunities for easy sociability and organized community life. These urban values are likely to be especially important to young adults, couples without children, and those highly educated, upper-middle-class people who are strongly oriented to the distinctive cultural facilities of the city.

Even confirmed urban values may not suffice to keep people in the cities if the problems of deteriorating facilities, increasing inconvenience, and growing threats to public order and private well-being are not resolved. If these problems are not dealt with adequately, the population of the cities is likely to consist of those with incomes that enable them to transcend many of the difficulties of city living (often through second residences away from the city to which they can repair on occasion), those who cannot afford to move away from the city or buy a home in the suburbs, and those racial and ethnic minorities which are excluded from the suburbs even if they can afford to move there.

Whether cities will be able to deal with their increasing problems depends primarily upon public policy at all levels of government, as does the form that the suburbs will take and the relationships that develop between cities and suburbs. Urban problems and urban growth, though obviously affected by large-scale economic, social, and cultural trends, are no longer to be seen as the product of impersonal forces manifested in a myriad of largely uncontrollable individual actions. Institutionalized controls over land use, tax policies, public programs directed toward specific problems, and major decisions such as the location of a new highway, the building of a housing project, or the construction of a cultural center are clearly of strategic importance in determining the shape and form of cities, suburbs, and metropolitan areas. The urban future is, therefore, at least to some degree a matter of conscious choice and action.

The actions taken and the choices made will inevitably be constrained by those economic, social, and cultural facts which provide the context for public policy. Those engaged in formulating that policy—making the day-to-day decisions affecting urban growth and development, and planning for the future—must continuously deal with the problems generated by the present and emerging character and distribution of people, facilities, and activities. The scale, complexity, and variety of these problems have made them increasingly difficult to deal with, but there are several general issues underlying them that must be resolved as specific questions are attacked. First, what is to be the balance between dispersion and concentration? There seems little doubt that metropolitan areas will continue to grow and that in some parts of the United States the tendency toward megalopolis will persist. But within metropolitan (and megalopolitan) areas, is there to be a more or less even distribution of population and of economic and other activities, or will the cities continue to have higher population densities and a concentration of activities and facilities? If urban densities decline, as they already have in some places, and suburban numbers increase, will the entire metropolitan area come to resemble a giant collection of suburbs, or will suburban densities creep up toward those of the cities, bringing with them many of the problems that now afflict the cities?

Second, how are the various functions that are performed throughout the metropolitan area to be distributed? Will there continue to be some differentiation of functions among the various parts of the metropolitan area, allowing for diversity and variety within an integrated whole? Alternatively, will the area eventually become a number of more or less self-sufficient communities, each providing for most of the needs and wants of its residents, or will the entire area become a relatively homogeneous mass with residences, jobs, services, and facilities distributed throughout almost at random, like raisins in a pudding?

Third, will the city itself survive? Since many of the functions once confined to the city need no longer remain there, will affluence and mobility lead to the continuing decline of cities which, in the judgement of many observers, are no longer manageable or governable? Are those values inherent in city life and the economic interests built into its physical plant strong enough to ensure that the imagination and resources necessary for its survival —and revival—will eventually be committed to it?

The answers to these questions may well come by default, by the absence of any action to control or direct the form and character of urban society. If the underlying tendencies in metropolitan growth were to persist without conscious efforts to shape and direct them, the result, as noted earlier, would probably be festering and decaying cities and suburbs with increasing problems. Yet despite this prospect, there are serious and sometimes almost intractable obstacles to those actions that might resolve present problems and avoid even greater ones in the future.

The political system through which decisions must be made and actions taken in itself constitutes a major obstacle to the integrated effort and planning needed to deal with many of the problems of urban America. These problems cut across political boundaries, so that the definition of the appropriate level at which they should be attacked must continually be reexamined, while the number of political subdivisions within metropolitan areas and the complex relations among cities, states, and the federal government make it difficult to formulate and carry out effective programs at any level. Greater home rule and increased neighborhood autonomy within cities, though often useful and even necessary, may also make it more difficult to cope with those problems that encompass the entire metropolitan area or large segments within it. Similarly, the autonomy of the suburb, which allows for the civic participation valued by many suburban residents, may inhibit the larger actions needed to provide services and control growth. But metropolitan or regional government, in the various forms in which it has been proposed, runs the risk of losing touch with the problems of the smaller separate communities within the larger whole, and is now seen by many central city blacks as a threat to the political power their numbers may gain them.

Underlying these political problems are cultural perspectives that also present serious obstacles to effective action. American culture has always (except, perhaps, in time of war) placed greater emphasis upon the goals and desires of individuals than upon collective needs. Individual perspectives are likely to be confined to immediate personal aims rather than to those larger needs which must be satisfied if each member of the community is to be able to realize his goals. As a result, efforts to control the growth of the community or even to provide the services and facilities that only public authorities can provide are often inhibited, or even totally blocked. Each individual might be free to build a home wherever he chooses only to find a new highway running in front of his door; he may move away from the city in search of open space only to have a new housing development go up on the open fields near his home; he may drive his car wherever he chooses, only to discover that the volume of traffic slows him down or diminishes his pleasure, and that the number of cars destroys the quiet and befouls the air he breathes. The suburbanite, secure in his retreat from the city in which he earns his livelihood and to which he goes for recreation and pleasure, refuses to accept any responsibility for dealing with those problems that may eventually destroy the advantages he gains from the city.

Individualistic opposition to urban and regional planning and to the possibility of public action has, of course, been weakened though much remains to be done and strong resistence to effective measures persists. Moreover, there are still great differences in the solutions that are offered to the problems that beset the city and the metropolitan area as a whole. There are those who insist on the need to improve mass transportation, while others advocate more and better highways, more parking places, and rationalized traffic patterns that would allow the uninhibited use of the private automobile. Those who stress the need to dissolve racial ghettoes in the cities are opposed by residents of other neighborhoods who want to maintain their homogeneous communities. Supporters of a diversified city trying to increase the supply of middle-income housing often run into opposition from spokesmen for the poor who insist that new housing must be predominantly for low-income groups, particularly if it is in any way subsidized by the government. Advocates of a broader metropolitan government cutting across existing political boundaries oppose supporters of neighborhood autonomy, and both run into opposition from those who benefit from the existing distribution of power.

These disagreements obviously reflect the concrete interests that are involved, for different groups stand to gain or lose from different measures to control urban and suburban growth and to deal with the problems of urban America. But it is also caused by differing views as to what a community should—or might—be. We have already described the suburban pattern which now seems to be the prepotent image of community in America. If this pattern continues to predominate, unchallenged and without significant alternatives, it will become increasingly difficult to muster the resources necessary to maintain the city even in its present parlous state, and impossible to create cities that would become, as President Johnson put it in describing the long-range goals to which his urban program was to be dedicated, "the masterpieces of our civilization."

The city has always had its defenders and there are contemporary writers and planners—among them, John Burchard, Charles Abrams, Victor Gruen, and Jane Jacobs—who have tried to define and describe in contemporary terms what the city might become. But there persists in American culture a strong antiurban bias—an assumption that vice and corruption run rampart in the city, a suspicion of city slickers, an uneasiness in the city that is attributed to "artificiality" and anonymity, and a resentment of the minority groups that seek the promises of the city at a time when these promises cannot be adequately or easily redeemed. This bias, which is linked to persisting images of a heroic frontier, a rural idyll, an "Our Town," tends to counterbalance or outweigh the potential of the city and to reinforce the suburban pattern and the tendency toward dispersion and decentralization.

Even if such city problems as congestion and pollution, public violence, and physical decay were to be resolved, the balance of cultural attitudes thus remains heavily weighted against the city. The efforts and funds necessary to sustain or restore the city are consequently not likely to be forthcoming unless suburbanites, small town residents, and rural folk, who collectively greatly outnumber city dwellers, see the city as an important resource for themselves, offering an alternative way of life that is worth preserving, and maintaining valuable facilities and functions that might be lost if the city disintegrates.

As this uncertain contingency suggests, the future of the city and of urban America as a whole depends to a considerable extent upon the goals that American society sets for itself and the values to which it is committed. These goals and values are of course subject to conflict and change. Efforts to plan for the future will necessarily involve a clarification of goals and of alternatives as well as specification of appropriate and effective means to achieve predefined ends.

Under these circumstances, the social scientist finds himself in the uncertain dilemma that has always been his lot. Because he is concerned with trends and the underlying forces that are at work, his analysis almost inevitably takes on a deterministic—and in the case of the contemporary city, a pessimistic—cast. But he also becomes aware of the limits of his interpretations and of the possibilities that are open if one set of goals is accepted rather than another; is strong leadership emerges to marshal collective energies toward clearly articulated objectives; if unforeseen events do not vitiate the plans men make. Though there are always limits that the past imposes upon the future, there is also room for change, intelligence, creativity, and imagination, all of which must play a role in shaping the urban future.

NOTES

1. John Friedmann and John Miller, "The Urban Field." See chapter 3.
2. David Riesman, *Individualism Reconsidered* (Glencoe, Ill.: The Free Press, 1954), p. 476.
3. The 1969 figure is from United States Bureau of the Census, *Current Population Reports,* Series P–20, No. 197 (Washington, D.C.: U.S. Government Printing Office). The 1968 figure is from *Current Population Reports,* Series P–25, No. 432.
4. *Current Population Reports,* Series P–25, No. 432.
5. Jean Gottman, *Megalopolis* (New York: The Twentieth Century Fund, Inc., 1961).
6. *Current Population Reports,* Series P–25, No. 381.
7. Cited in William Alonso, "The Mirage of New Towns," *The Public Interest,* No. 19 (Spring, 1970), p. 5.
8. Patricia Leavey Hodge and Philip M. Hauser, *The Challenge of America's Metropolitan Population Outlook, 1960 to 1985.* Prepared for the National Commission on Urban Problems (New York: Praeger, 1968).
9. John M. Kain, "The Distribution and Movement of Jobs and Industry," in James Q. Wilson (ed.), *The Urban Enigma* (Cambridge, Mass.: Harvard University Press, 1968), p. 28.
10. See Wendell Bell, "Social Choice, Life Styles, and Suburban Residence," in William Dobriner (ed.), *The Suburban Community* (New York: G. P. Putnam's Sons, 1958), pp. 225–47.
11. Herbert Gans, *The Levittowners* (New York: Pantheon, 1967), p. 38.
12. See Leo Lowenthal, "Biographies in Popular Magazines," in William Petersen (ed.), *American Social Patterns* (Garden City, N.Y.: Doubleday Anchor Books, 1956).

1 *The Transformation of the Urban Community*

YORK WILLBERN

In this largely historical account, York Willbern, Professor of Political Science at Indiana University, describes the double revolution in urban society. First came the dense concentration of people in cities, then their dispersal, with their urban way of life, across the countryside. By identifying some of the forces that operate in both revolutions he clarifies the alternatives that are open, though he concludes that the future may find urban America resembling "a thin layer of scrambled eggs spread over much of the platter."

The linguistic and historical relationships between the words "city" and "civilization" have often been noted. The present state of American cities and that great part of the civilization of this country which revolves around their functioning and well-being, have provoked a rapidly growing volume of interest and concern.

Most literate people are reasonably familiar with the gross outlines of urban population movements. They know that urban areas have increased in population much more rapidly than rural areas, that the great bulk of this growth has been in areas of metropolitan character, and that suburban areas have been growing much more rapidly than have central cities. None of us, however, yet understands adequately the implications and consequences of these massive redistributions of the population.

We are participating, in my opinion, in two revolutions, one imposed upon the other, and the meaning of the second is partially obscured by the fact that the first, much older, revolution is continuing even as the second develops.

The first of these revolutions, of course, is the rise of an urban way of life. The second is its diffusion and dispersal over the countryside. The first has been in the making in Europe and in this country for several hundred years. It was in nearly full flower when Johnson and Boswell were enjoying the fleshpots of eighteenth century London. This revolution was based on the rise of trade and on the growth of industry. The new technologies which promoted specialization, manufacturing, and great increases in the interchange of goods and services have continued and been accelerated in the last two generations. They are now world-wide in their impact; the non-Western world as well as the West is struggling today with the gains and costs of these changes. Those who are staggered by the problems of urbanization in this country are really shaken when they see Tokyo or Calcutta. Tokyo, the world's most populous city, has no sewerage for eighty per cent of the metropolitan area. In Calcutta two-thirds of a million people have no home but the public streets and alleys.[1]

These urbanizing forces continue unabated in this country. The proportion of the national population living in areas defined by the Census Bureau as "metropolitan" increased from 58 per cent in 1950 to 63 per cent in 1960. The proportions continue to grow and will probably reach 70 to 75 per cent before the Census Bureau decides that it is unable any longer to fabricate definitions to demarcate a population which is almost universally metropolitanized.

The second revolution is much newer and has been much more strongly felt in this country than anywhere else. This is the outward explosion of our urban centers. It has several causes, of course. One is the desire of families, particularly families with children, for detached dwellings on substantial plots of land. Sir

Frederic J. Osborn, dean of British planners and editor of *Town and Country Planning,* emphasized this desire in a recent address to American planning officials, and in so doing raised a question of crucial importance to the continuation and welfare of large cities. He indicated that the most disastrous shortcoming associated with city size is "the lack of sufficient space inside cities for good family dwellings with private yards or gardens, for recreation, for industrial efficiency, and for the vegetative surroundings and the quiet and simple beauty man needs and desires for the fullness of life."

> Relative unconsciousness of this aspect of the urban problem surprises me in all countries, including my own, because the most conspicuous cause of the "metropolitan explosion" is the spontaneous quest by more and more urban families, as net incomes rise, for the family house standing in its own yard. The outward movement of the well-off is nothing new; what is new is the spread of wealth to far more numerous classes who can afford what Susannah's husband provided for her in Babylon and great senators took for themselves in ancient Rome—a suburban home in a garden. . . . such environments reflect a universal natural desire that man indulges wherever and whenever he becomes prosperous and free.
>
> Admittedly, there are some genuine addicts of high urban culture to whom space and green surroundings make little appeal—types who like to live in city centres with their rich assemblies of theatres, concert halls, art galleries, restaurants, night clubs, snack bars, and hamburger stands—and are reassured by the bustle of crowds, traffic noises, flashing signs, and the insistent impact on their senses of commercial vitality. I do not deplore the existence of these types, though I suspect that their contribution to our culture is over valued. But they are a tiny minority. . . .[2]

This view is, of course, greatly at odds with that suggested by Mrs. Jane Jacobs in a book which is currently attracting a great deal of attention among students of urbanism.[3] If the figures on population movement are an accurate indication of the desires of people for home environments, the evidence certainly supports Sir Frederic's view much more strongly than that of Mrs. Jacob .

A good many technological developments have made this dispersion of urban housing relatively easy. Reliance upon electric power and the ease of power transmission, telephone lines, septic tanks and similar developments bring to widely scattered houses many of the conveniences and amenities once possible only in very closely settled cities.

A development of social technology—the long-term, monthly payment mortgage loan with low interest rates—has greatly facilitated the spread of American families into single-family detached dwellings. The growth of credit arrangements of this type has certainly been encouraged and fostered by national legislation. It can be argued that the nature of the urban residential patterns of this generation has been shaped very substantially by FHA and similar governmental programs. The overwhelming political support for these programs, however, and the existence of parallel nongovernmental developments indicate clearly that these credit socialization devices have probably been more the product than the cause of the social and economic forces at work.

If the basic desire for detached dwellings and space is one cause of the dispersion, another and very important cause is the appearance and practically universal use of the automobile in this country. We now have available, for most individuals, personalized rapid transit. The customary reaction to the automobile of Mrs. Jacobs and others who admire the congestion of dense urban settlement is to wish it would go away.

The impact of the automobile revolution is newer than many of us realize; its outlines are only now beginning to emerge. The last decade [1950–1960] was the first in which it was fully operative; the 1960 census returns gave figures which indicate some of the results on a nationwide basis. Automobiles began to be widespread in the 1920s, but too little time had as yet passed for really basic changes in ways of living and spatial relationships. In the 1930s the great economic depression overshadowed and hampered adjustments to the new technology; the 1940s brought another overpowering circumstance, the war and its aftermath, to mask and postpone the basic changes. They hit us full force in the 1950s, but a decade is a short time for a social revolution. The greatest public works enterprise in the history of mankind, our national system of expressways, which will probably give the automobile age its greatest boost since the Model T Ford, is just beginning. I am indebted to Harlan Cleveland for a statistic which he considered the most interesting of a recent year: we now have enough automotive vehicles in operation in this country for every man, woman, and child in the population to ride comfortably and simultaneously in the front seats.

It is difficult for us to realize that this new revolution may have a social impact comparable to that of the first. The basic purpose of a city is the facilitation of interchange—the interchange of goods through trade and merchandising, of labor and services in industrial and service enterprises, of messages and ideas in financial and political and cultural activities. When the means of interchange are drastically altered, the nature of the city must also be drastically altered.

In the large cities of a century ago, population was tightly concentrated. Concentration was necessary, in order for people to get from home to work and school and shop and engage in the other complex exchanges of a city. When each individual and most of the goods move from place to place within the urban environment in a vehicle weighing more than a ton and capable of moving economically at the rate of a mile a minute, the old patterns of settlement are technologically obsolete and will inevitably be changed. To achieve for a given population the same facility of circulation that the older concentrated cities had for pedestrian, horse-drawn, or even rail traffic, the modern city requires a land area many times greater. When movement and interchange were pedestrian and horse-drawn, an efficient area for a population of 200,000 might be about four square miles;[4] for 200,000 people now, on a one or two persons per car basis (increasingly the normal pattern), the most efficient area might well be 100 square miles.

Many of the great cities of the world outside the United States are experiencing the integrating revolution, with relatively little evidence yet of the disintegrating one. Perhaps they may avoid the second. A Soviet economist, watching Americans coming to work one-in-a-car is supposed to have said "we'll never make that mistake—that is, if we can help it."[5]

In this country, however, disintegrating forces are moving at a rapid pace. The area north of the Ohio River and east from Chicago and St. Louis contains the urban heart of the United States. There were in this area in 1950 a dozen cities with more than half a million inhabitants each. What happened to the population of these cities in the decade of the 1950s, a decade in which urbanization continued apace? Every one of them lost, rather than gained, in population. While the urban area, the metropolitan area, in each case grew very substantially in population, not a single one of the large central cities in this area increased. If this is what is happening to the oldest, best established American cities, will Birmingham and Indianapolis, or even Houston and Los Angeles, be far behind?

The famous Regional Plan of 1929 for the New York metropolitan area projected a population by 1965 of 21 million people living in approximately 1,000 square miles of the region. In 1960, five years before the projected date, there were actually only 16 million people but the urbanized area constituted 2,000 square miles, twice the projected amount.[6]

The most recent major study of the New York metropolitan area, which Raymond Vernon and his associates made for the same Regional Plan Association, came to the following conclusion:

> As one surveys the outward shift of the population in the New York Metropolitan Region and of the consumer activities tied to them, the forces behind the shift seem near-inexorable. Basic technological developments in transportation and deepseated changes in consumer wants appear to lie behind the phenomenon. Here and there one sees evidences of preferences which breast the main tide; the occasional reappearance of a disillusioned exurbanite in his former city haunts, the gradual growth of apartments-in-the-city for the very rich—these are phenomena whose impact cannot be overlooked. The bigger risk, however, is that their implications for the future will be exaggerated rather than

TABLE 1.1: *Change in Population, 1950-1960, Major Cities in Northeast and Midwest*

	1950	*1960*	*Amount Change*
Baltimore	949,708	939,024	— 10,684
Boston	801,444	697,197	—104,247
Buffalo	580,132	532,759	— 47,373
Chicago	3,620,962	3,550,404	— 70,558
Cincinnati	503,998	502,550	— 1,448
Cleveland	914,808	876,050	— 38,758
Detroit	1,849,568	1,670,144	—179,424
New York	7,891,957	7,781,984	—109,973
Philadelphia	2,071,605	2,002,512	— 69,093
Pittsburgh	676,806	604,332	— 72,474
St. Louis	856,796	750,026	—106,770
Washington, D.C.	802,178	763,956	— 38,222

Source: *Statistical Abstract of the United States,* 1962, pp. 22–23.

overlooked. Short of some fundamental alteration in consumer outlook or in urban environment, the trends for the future seem likely to represent a continuation—even a speed up—of the dispersive tendencies of the past.[7]

This is what they predict in the text of the book. After coming to this conclusion, however, Mr. Vernon inspected the 1960 census returns and found that he had been short of the mark. The city core has declined in population more than he anticipated, and the outlying areas have expanded more rapidly. In a footnote attached after the report was completed, but before the volume was finally published, he confessed that "in general, the dispersive population forces in the Region seem even stronger than those built into our model."[8]

Even the census figures summarizing the growth in the outlying portions of metropolitan areas and the losses or much slower growth in the urban core may understate the dispersion. For example, the Census Bureau defines the Indianapolis metropolitan area as Marion County. This area increased in population by 24 percent between 1950 and 1960, a very substantial rate of growth. But the countries immediately to the north, east, south, and west of Marion County, not included in the census-defined metropolitan area, had rates of growth of 40, 30, 67, and 65 per-cent, respectively. The growth of these counties immediately beyond the census metropolitan area limits is not considered in the statistics to be suburban growth, but the percentage growth has often been even greater than that of the suburban areas *within* the official metropolitan area.

During the decades when the urbanizing forces were strongest, and before the forces of dispersal had begun to accumulate, the percentage of the population living in the central city of an urbanizing area increased substantially. This percentage has tended to decrease as the second revolution has become mixed with the first. In Figure 1.1 are some representative figures from three cities at which I have been looking intensively.

In each of the three cities the central city reached its peak percentage in 1920 or 1930, along with the initial surge of the automobile revolution, and has since declined at a rapid and ordinarily accelerating rate. New York City constituted the largest percentage, in population, of the countries composing its metropolitan area in 1910; the percentage has been dropping ever since. The peak in Birmingham was 1930.

In gross national figures the greatest concentration of metropolitan population inside central cities occurred between 1920 and 1930. Until 1920 the central cities were growing faster than their metropolitan rings; beginning with the census of 1930, the fringe growth has been faster than the central growth, and the gap widens with each census. During the 1950–1960 decade, the central cities of the 212 metropolitan areas of the country increased 1.5 per cent in population within their 1950 boundaries, and added another 9.2 per cent by annexation, for a total increase of 10.7 per cent, and, as I have indicated, many of the biggest and oldest actually lost population. The remaining, or fringe portion of the metropolitan areas, increased 48.6 per cent. The more than ninety percent of the land area outside the metropolises saw its population increase by eleven percent.

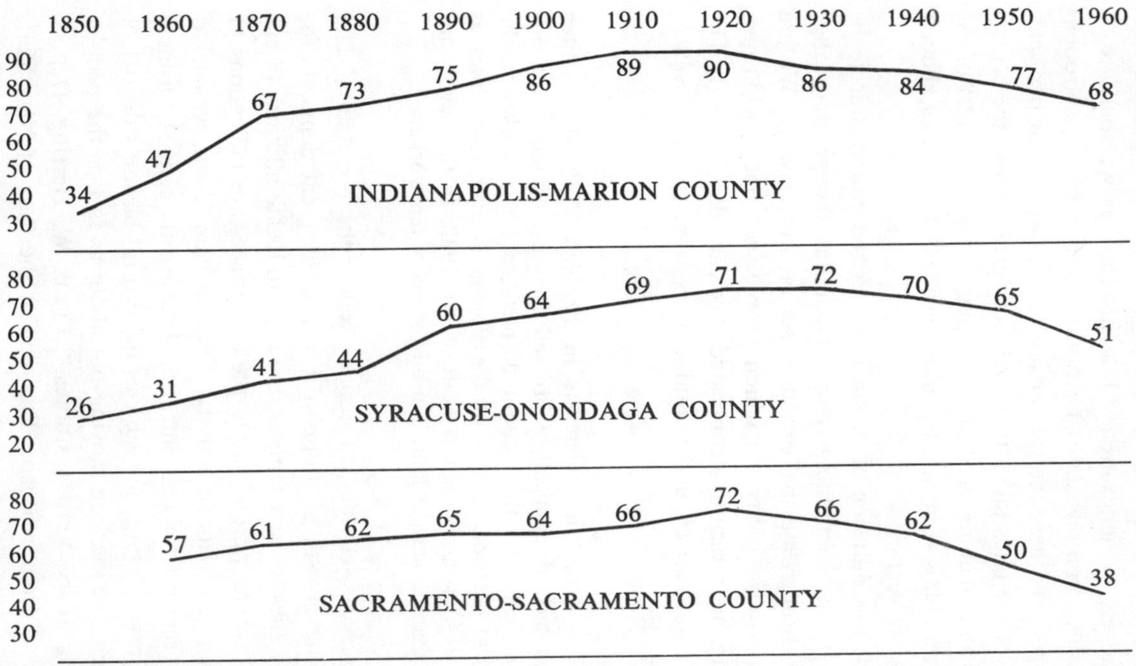

FIGURE 1.1: *Percentage of County Population in Central City, Three Cities, 1850-1960*

It is roughly accurate to say that one-third of the American population is within the central cities of metropolitan areas, and this segment is increasing at the rate of 1 per cent per year, almost entirely by annexation. (This increase, as we shall see, is concentrated in a few states.) Another third is in the metropolitan fringes, and here the rate of increase is 4 per cent per year, in spite of the bites taken from it by annexation into the central cities. The remaining third of the population is in the rest of the country, and this segment also is increasing at the rate of about 1 per cent per year.

Nor is this diffusion of urban life over the countryside to be limited by the commuting range, expanding though that range may be through massive expenditures on expressways. We are not witnessing a pattern in which people seek out spaciousness for living, but return to a congested core each day for work. The jobs also seek space, and manufacturers want space as well as home builders.

> In recent years, manufacturers in the New York Metropolitan Region have dramatically increased their use of land. Our surveys indicate that the amount of plot space per worker in the post war suburban plants of the Region is over four times as great as in suburban plants built before 1922. In the new plants more than an acre of land is used for every ten workers.[9]

The service activities, of course, follow the population. The spectacular growth of shopping centers, the great demands for extensive sites for new schools, the need to locate all kinds of enterprises where there is ample parking space, are indications of dispersion in economic activity. Even in New York, which has peculiar reasons for concentration because its central business district serves in large measure as the central business district of the nation, the jobs are moving out about as fast as the people, according to the Vernon studies.[10] Frank W. Herring, Deputy Director of Comprehensive Planning of the Port of New York Authority, says that "growth in journey-to-work travel is no longer focused on the Central Business District, but rather is characterized by intersuburban travel, reverse commuting and the like."[11]

The net flow of commuting is, of course, still toward the center, and it will probably continue to be for a long time. The Vernon studies indicate that the core of the New York area now has about half the population of the region and two-thirds of the jobs. According to their projections, by 1985 the core will have only one-third the population but will probably still have half the jobs.

The dispersion of employment may be greater in other centers than in New York. In the Chicago area (where the city of Chicago constitutes a larger portion of its metropolitan area than does New York), the city's share of manufacturing employment in the area fell from 84 per cent in 1920 to 81 per cent in 1940 and to 72 per cent in 1957.[12] A continuation of this accelerating trend would suggest that the city of Chicago now has less than 70 per cent of the industrial jobs in the area, compared to about 58 per cent of the people.

> Dispersal of manufacturing activity from the inner zones of the central city was the dominant trend in plant location throughout the United States in 1950–1960. In Chicago, typically, the greatest gains in activity took place in an arc ten to fifteen miles from the central business district. The greatest losses occurred within five miles of the core. Warehouses, in particular, moved from inner zones to the periphery, situating themselves close to areas of population growth and expanded manufacturing activity. To call this process suburbanization may be too much of a simplification.[13]

In many cities of smaller size, the great developments in industrialization, and in jobs, occur beyond the city limits. The new industries tend to locate in industrial parks, or on spacious sites well outside the cities. In Syracuse, New York, for example, the city's proportion of the population of Onondaga County has been declining for more than twenty years, but its proportion of the assessed valuation of the county has been declining even more rapidly than its proportion of the population, indicating that productive property, which has higher assessments than residences, has been growing faster outside the city than inside.[14]

Some observers argue that the tide of movement out of central cities into suburban and urban areas can be checked and reversed by improved mass transit, renewal of the older urban areas, and various other remedial measures. Efforts in this direction may be expected to continue. It seems likely that policy changes may affect the character of the movement somewhat, but the overwhelming bulk of the evidence makes the outward movement seem, as Vernon and his associates put it in their study of New York, "inexorable."

Most of our accumulated physical capital is in urban areas. The sweeping changes in the technology of settlement and interchange which have resulted in the shifting populations have a great impact on the maintenance and utility of these accumulated investments. The existence of these great investments, both in physical facilities and in skills and habits, constitutes a great drag upon adaptation to technological innovation. Farm homes and land holdings and habits of work have continued long after becoming technologically obsolescent; this is the basic cause of our so-called "farm problem." We now have similar lags because of the investments in outmoded urban plants. We live, however, in a relatively affluent age, an age when we can make massive continuing new investments, even at the price of losing full use of much of the old. Furthermore, our society is increasingly mobile, not only geographically but in capacity to shift patterns of behavior. Substitution of investment for many reasons, in addition to the changing technology of communication and movement, goes on continually.

With new investments being made as a matter of course, the investors (whether in productive plant, or in patterns of service, or in housing and ways of life) are able to locate in better conformity to the technological patterns of the present and future. The pressures to maintain and adapt and renew the center which have characterized European cities for many generations are far less demanding here. A merchant who sees opportunities for growth in an expanding urban environment, and who has or can get capital to invest, is much less likely to use it in rebuilding or refurnishing and improving a downtown store location. Instead he will join a new regional shopping center near a freeway interchange where there can be six square feet of parking space for every square foot of selling space.

So far, in this country the forces of the second, suburbanizing revolution have been balanced in large measure by the continuing forces of the first, urbanizing revolution. The massive forces for dispersal of investment have been accompanied by such great need for the use of all the possible capital available in urban areas that both the new and much of the old have been necessary.

The physical decay and obsolescence of the older investment have not yet resulted in great decreases in property values. In the last thirty years the rate of investment in new housing units and new industrial and business sites in urban areas has not exceeded the rate of influx from the remote rural communities. To be more explicit, although over a million housing units a year have been built in urban fringe areas for the last decade, as yet comparatively few vacancies have appeared in the deteriorating housing units of the central cities. The new units serve as additions to the total urban supply, not as replacements. The accumulated overcrowding of the depression and war years and the continuing immigration from rural parts of the country have kept the demand for housing units at a sufficient intensity that rental income from slum property is still highly remunerative. As fast as the inhabitants of the gray area (or "mice country," as Robert Wood calls it) have moved out to the suburbs, the Negro, Puerto Rican, and hill country farm people have crowded in to the decaying houses of the old city. Reductions in population of the central cities, now definitely begun, have made it possible so far only to clear some land to provide more room for automobiles to maneuver and be stored and to reduce somewhat the doubling up and overcrowding; vacancy rates in slum housing are still not high enough to worry the landlords.

There are some indications that new housing construction has begun to catch up with the urban population growth. As to the deteriorating central city housing in New York, Vernon suggests that "no projection which we would consider realistic contemplates an increase in the demand for such housing in the Region anywhere near as great as the prospective increase in supply."[15] If vacancies in the slums begin to mount (as is already true in some decaying commercial and industrial properties) reductions in income potential may cause the values of the decaying central city properties to fall significantly.

Some forces do exist which tend to offset the disintegrating effects of transportation changes and the desire of people for detached dwellings. One is the great value for many small enterprises of what the economists call "external economies." These are the specialist services which a large enterprise may provide for itself but which a small enterprise can best get from other suppliers. Although these may be interchanged even in a dispersed, less congested locational pattern, there remain some advantages in the greater proximity of denser locations.

Second, and much more important, some activities in our complex society are best carried on where there is frequent and convenient opportunity for face-to-face contact with a variety of other people: the financial institutions, for example; the central corporate offices; the advertising business. Here, intelligence is perhaps the chief item of exchange, and it can best be exchanged on the basis of frequent conferences, luncheons, and personal contacts. For this reason the shining towers of central Manhattan continue to rise although much of the surrounding area is deteriorating.

The central business district of New York has peculiar advantages, of course, because it performs so many of these functions for the whole nation and even the world. At the same time, the proportion of our society engaged in the white-collar, highly interpersonal communication activities is increasing so extensively that there are good economic prospects for the core of central business districts of many of our cities, even though the fabrication and distribution of goods may be continually dispersed.

Third, some industries need large quantities of relatively low-wage labor. Since the lowest income groups tend to live in the central city, and relatively near the center, and since these groups are somewhat less mobile, it is sometimes advantageous for lower-wage industries to stay near the population and transit center. In Chicago the industries showing the lowest decentralizing tendencies (though even here the net movement was outward) were textiles and apparel, lumber and furniture, and food products, all of which are comparatively low-wage operations.[16]

A fourth centralizing factor may be suggested, but its actual impact is not easy to predict. This is the almost certain great increase in the number of two-house families. Two-car families are now commonplace in this country, and two-house families are expected to become so. Already perhaps a million of the fifty million family units have more than one place of residence, and these million tend to be the high-income, high-status families whose patterns of life are copied by others as quickly as they can afford it. If one residence offers almost complete isolation, many families may plump in favor of the attractions and conveniences of high-density living for the other residence and use their automobiles as much or more for weekend as for daily commuting. The apparent preference of people with children for detached dwellings, however, along with the continually growing reliance upon the automobile even for frequent movements during the day, leads to considerable doubt that the rise in dual dwellings will result in more than a marginal integrating force.

How much can public policy shape and guide and direct these patterns of investment and of settlement? Was it government's cheap land policy which led to the rapid agricultural expansion of the early nineteenth century, or did migration and settlement force the government to follow the policy it did? Was it governmental promotion of the transcontinental railroads later in the century, and the Panama Canal early in this century, that linked the two coasts into an economic unit, or did the economic ties and links make the governmental public works enterprises necessary? Was it the massive public water system that made possible the settlement of so many people in and around New York, and the development and operation of the subway system that enabled them to focus such a concentration of economic activity in Manhattan, or were these great public enterprises produced rather haltingly to meet the necessities of the developing situation? No simple answer is possible to such chicken-and-egg priority questions, but recent searching economic studies of metropolitan regions suggest very strongly that, as Charles Adrian summarizes it:

> Both local and regional (metropolitan) governments tend to follow the economic pattern rather than to lead it. Governmental innovations that complement the decisions of the market place are likely to succeed; others are not. [17]

The British have had the urbanizing revolution for a longer period and to a greater degree than we have, and the early waves of a flood of urban dispersal (they call it urban sprawl) are apparent in England today. Between 1952 and 1960 the population of the London conurbation decreased by 139,000, while the population of the twenty to thirty mile wide belt encircling the conurbation increased by 765,000. But only the people are moving out—not the jobs. The center gained 260,000 jobs while losing 140,000 residents; the fringe gained only 200,000 jobs while acquiring 750,000 inhabitants.[18] The British planners have urged, and partially implemented, a national policy to combat both the congestion of the center and the sprawl of the cutting edges. They propose to constrict the central metropolis with an encircling green belt and to take care of the "over spill" in new towns—either completely new or planned new developments around old but small centers. The density of the great central cities is gradually to be reduced. Each of the new towns is to be relatively self-contained, with jobs for the inhabitants, trade and service establishments to care for their needs, appropriate community facilities, and adequate housing, all located within a space convenient to pedestrian or bicycle mobility. To keep this convenience of access, the new towns are to have firm limits as to size, and while most houses will be single-family with small garden spaces, residential densities will be substantially higher than in most American suburban developments.

Many American planners favor exploring similar programs in this country, but they are hampered by great technological and economic obstacles. Whatever the case in Britain, it is difficult to foresee here a relationship between place of residence and place of employment stable enough to make the self-contained, small-city concept a viable one. American occupational and residential mobility creates too many opportunities for the worker to find more attractive employment in another city or in the central metropolis without moving his residence. Or he can find more attractive housing in another place without changing jobs. With the ubiquity of the automobile and the high-speed road, the population will not be "contained." Furthermore, the needs of the automobile for space will almost certainly dictate much more extensive patterns of land utilization than are foreseen by the British.

Even in Britain there are substantial doubts that the scheme can withstand the assault of growing affluence and motorization. Some big industrial establishments, located on the outskirts of the metropolitan areas, are recruiting workers in some of the new towns. This tendency, if pushed much further, may make of some of them bedroom suburbs for commuters. Some of the shopping centers in the new towns are so attractive that they draw automobile-borne customers from great distances around, and thus become regional shopping centers after the American pattern, but without the facilities for parking or traffic-handling. While the new town developments certainly have many attractions, political pressure has not been great enough to induce the government to build them at anything like the rate which the planners would like. And even in the green belts, though they have been relatively well protected, the pressures for land are so great that the rate of development and of population growth exceeds the national and the urban averages.

Whatever may be the situation in other countries, the evidence seems clear that in this country our farms and small towns are being abandoned in a great movement into an urban way of life. At the same time the city, in the sense of a tightly-knit corporate community with a clear distinction between its high-density living and the rural countryside, is fast becoming so blurred at the edges as to be incapable of operational definition. There seems little to block an endless expansion of urban or semi-urban ways of life over vast areas of the countryside outside our traditional city limits. Instead of distinct cities with distinguishable centers and edges somewhat like a fried egg, we seem likely to be approaching in large segments of our country a condition somewhat like that of a thin layer of scrambled eggs spread over much of the platter. The more urban we become, the more shaky become both the concept and the reality of the city.

NOTES

1. *New York Times,* 17 December, 1961, p. 40; Paul N. Ylvisaker, address to the World Traffic Engineering Conference, Washington, D.C., August 21, 1961.
2. Frederic J. Osborn, "The Conqueror City," *Town and Country Planning,* XXIX (April, 1961), 141.
3. Jane Jacobs, *The Death and Life of Great American Cities* (New York: Random House, 1961).
4. In 1850 Philadelphia had a population of 121,000 and an area of two square miles.
5. Ylvisaker, p. 18.
6. Paul Windels, "The Region—Past, Present, and Future," *Metropolis 1985,* p. 21, a report from a conference held at Arden House, March 1, 1961.
7. Raymond Vernon, *Metropolis 1985* (Cambridge: Harvard University Press, 1960), p. 165.
8. *Ibid.,* p. 222.
9. *Ibid.,* pp. 116–117.
10. New York is to be contrasted to London and Tokyo, its two largest competitors as world urban centers. In both of these, the population increase is at the edges while the jobs continue to be relatively contrated in the center. Paul Ylvisaker reports that land in the heart of Tokyo is four times as expensive as land in the heart of Manhattan. The chief reason for the defference is almost certainly the difference in the state of the automotive revolution.
11. "Metropolitan Growth and Metropolitan Travel Patterns," a paper presented at the annual meeting of the Highway Research Board, Committee on Urban Research, January 12, 1961.
12. Northeastern Illinois Metropolitan Area Planning Commission, *Social Geography of Metropolitan Chicago* (Chicago, 1960), p. 20.
13. Mark Reinsberg, *Growth and Change in Metropolitan Areas and Their Relation to Metropolitan Transportation: A Research Summary* (Evanston, Ill.: The Transportation Center, Northwestern University, 1961), p. 10.

14. Roscoe C. Martin et al, *Decisions in Syracuse* (Bloomington: Indiana University Press, 1961) pp. 23 and 29.
15. Vernon, p. 154.
16. Reinsberg, pp. 18–19.
17. Charles R. Adrian, "Metropology: Folklore and Field Research," *Public Administration Review,* XXI (Summer, 1961), 155.
18. "The London Region and the Development of South East England, 1961 to 1981," *Town and Country Planning,* XXIX (June, 1961), 225.

2 *The Form and Structure of the Future Urban Complex*

CATHERINE BAUER WURSTER

In this essay, Mrs. Wurster, a writer and critic on architecture, housing, and planning and, at the time of her death, Professor of City and Regional Planning at the University of California, Berkeley, outlines "a range of alternatives for the spatial organization of the future urban complex". The two central coordinates, in her view, are dispersion-concentration and specialization-integration. The former refers to the extent to which persons and activities are distributed throughout the metropolitan region, the latter to the organization of functions within the region. The alternatives she outlines include merely the projection of present trends, with their varied and unclear pattern, general dispersion, concentrated super-cities, and "a constellation of relatively diversified and integrated cities." Which alternative will emerge clearly depends upon the kinds of policies that are followed with respect to such matters as transportation, housing, taxes, and planning.

Traditionally, an urban community was a city, and the nature of a city was obvious. In a limited space it brought together a wide variety of people; it made them accessible to one another, provided them with communication with the outside world, and stimulated them to engage in many kinds of specialized but interdependent activity. The city had a government whose essential functions were to resolve the people's differences in the common interest and to provide their necessary services. The city was a little world and its tight-knit, articulated form reflected its structural unity.

From Lowdon Wingo, Jr. (ed.), *Cities and Space*, pp. 73–101. Baltimore: The Johns Hopkins Press for Resources for the Future, Inc., 1963. Reprinted by permission of the publisher.

Modern metropolitan trends have destroyed the traditional concept of urban structure, and there is no new image to take its place. Blind forces push in various directions, while urban environments are being shaped by decisions which are neither based on any real understanding of cause-and-effect nor geared to consistent purposes. But the problems are steadily mounting, and all levels of government are called in to solve them. Public actions and expenditures of many kinds play an ever-increasing role in shaping the urban and regional environment. But the problems cannot be solved piecemeal by *ad hoc* decisions unrelated to any clear consensus about public purposes. Costly conflicts must be resolved, alternative directions identified, and the nature of the big choices, which tend to come in packages, thoroughly understood.

Efforts to develop effective concepts and criteria for modern urban organization, and to create new public images of the desirable metropolitan community, have come from various sources. Utopian ideas have had considerable influence, from the old Garden City movement which produced the British New Towns program to the reaction against all forms of decentralization reflected in the current zeal to "save the central cities" by local renewal programs, a kind of inverted or anti-Utopian Utopia. But the much less romantic push for effective metropolitan planning is finally focusing attention on the basic questions of urban form and structure in the United States, in various ways. The practical requirements of transportation planning have brought scientific methods of systems analysis and computer techniques into the development of alternative models for metropolitan growth and change, most advanced in the Penn-Jersey project. The equally practical requirements of public communication have stimulated such schemes as the Year 2000 Plan for the National Capital Region which dramatizes the problems and possibilities of future growth by presenting clear-cut alternative patterns. Finally, in the academic retreats, there is a fresh if belated wave of interest in theoretical explorations of the metropolitan wilderness, exemplified in the pioneering contributions of Walter Isard,

Jean Gottmann, Lloyd Rodwin, Kevin Lynch, Stuart Chapin, and Melvin Webber.

This essay falls into none of these categories. It espouses no specific goals, Utopian or otherwise, nor does it promote any particular program of public action. It tries to be reasonably objective and more or less systematic in suggesting a range of alternatives for the spatial organization of the future urban complex, with some of their possible implications. But neither the arguments nor the evidence pretend to be "scientific"; they are simply an array of ideas, opinions, facts, and hunches.

The Present Approach

Even accepting these limitations, it proved to be a difficult task to suggest viable choices for future urban organization, briefly yet with some degree of logic and comparative interpretation. The following approach is no more than a brave experiment, but it does hang on a fairly clear-cut set of premises which should at least provide some basis for argument. Since my concern throughout is with urban form and urban structure, essentially as a pair of dimensions, my use of the terms should be defined. "Form" means the physical pattern of land use, population distribution, and service networks, while "structure" signifies the spatial organization of human activities and interrelationships.

Underlying Assumptions: A Pair of Key Variables

In a discussion of "practical" alternatives, it is necessary to begin with the trends and forces that seem to be shaping present patterns. Then one can try to diagnose the major issues and the potential for change: problems, conflicts, shifting goals and values, new tools, which together might alter the course of environment-shaping decisions in various ways, leading toward different types of form and structure. Alternatives can then be suggested, with some of their possible implications. In other words, the test of viability must rest on judgments about the dynamic drives behind the development process, however difficult they may be to assess.

The trends and issues in metropolitan patterns of land use and communication seem to relate primarily to a pair of variables which can be loosely considered co-ordinates, one a rough key to "form," the other to "structure." The first falls along a scale which ranges from extreme dispersion to extreme concentration in space of urban activities and artifacts. This is the obvious metropolitan dichotomy: the tendency of certain functions to spread out horizontally over huge areas, while other functions pile up together. I have assumed that the major force behind dispersion is the propensity to seek "private" space values, a push which has been amplified by automobility and the increase in long-distance communication. Concentration, on the other hand, indicates close-knit physical linkages at the expense of private space. This may reflect purposeful choice, for example in office skyscrapers, or simply the lack of any other choice, as is often the case for low-income and minority residence.

The other variable is more difficult to characterize in simple terms, because the issue is seldom clearly posed although it is fundamental for all metropolitan planning. Indeed, the continuing controversy between the "decentrists" and the Big City defenders comes down to this question: at what physical scale can (or should) a significant degree of integration take place among the various specialized activities and functions of a regional complex? Specialization implies interdependence, with more or less coherent organization at one or more levels, for urban areas as well as for industrial production. The questions are: where, at what scale, and for what purposes?

These are obviously very complex questions, since the realms for various types and degrees of interaction and interdependence extend all the way from the house and the neighborhood with their limited domestic functions, to the nation, the world, and the universe. Let us agree, however, that the city was traditionally an important and relatively balanced realm for a certain set of functions in that it provided a varied population with housing, employment, and other frequently used and essential services. Most of these functions are still performed within a metropolitan area, but individual cities tend to be more and more specialized, serving a limited range of populations and activities. So the questions are: Do the pieces fit together only at the metropolitan level no matter what its size, or are there limitations of scale for certain everyday urban functions? Is the implicit assumption of most metropolitan transportation plans substantiated—that the metropolis is essentially a single diversified market for housing, jobs, and leisure-time facilities? Or is relatively balanced and integrated development feasible or desirable within metropolitan subareas? This is the premise behind proposals for New Towns or relatively self-sufficient satellite communities, and for more housing in the central city suited to the tastes and resources of middle- and upper-income people who work there.

This variable ranges from the metropolitan Super-City—a single system with highly differentiated and interdependent parts, through various transmutations to a group of smaller urban communities, each providing for most of the ordinary economic and social needs of an approximate cross-section of the urban population. This factor has obvious implications for governmental structure and social relations as well as for functional organization.

Selected Alternatives and Some Qualifications

This pair of variables, viewed as co-ordinates, suggests a wide range of hypothetical choices for future form and structure. In practical terms, however, an assessment of current trends, countertrends, and the forces behind them leads to the selection of four possibilities. They would not all be equally possible everywhere, and certain limitations should be noted at the outset. The stage of growth is a constraint: the form and scale of past development in a large old community, and the strengths of vested interests, are likely to impede any radical change in spatial organization, as compared with a relatively new metropolis most of whose growth is yet to come. The choices open to New York will be different from those for Los Angeles, Denver, or Sacramento, owing to the differences in what is there already and in the probable rates of future expansion.

The dominant functions of the region will limit choice, as will its particular endowment of resources: wealth, knowledge, energy, and ability, existing natural or man-made attractions; the area and character of land available for new development and redevelopment; the capacity for effective action toward common ends, via market and political processes.

Finally, whatever the local variables, the alternatives are more a matter of pursuing a fairly consistent course toward a certain set of goals than of achieving any particular kind of community in neat, pure form. The development of an entirely new urban agglomeration of major proportions is unlikely, though not im-

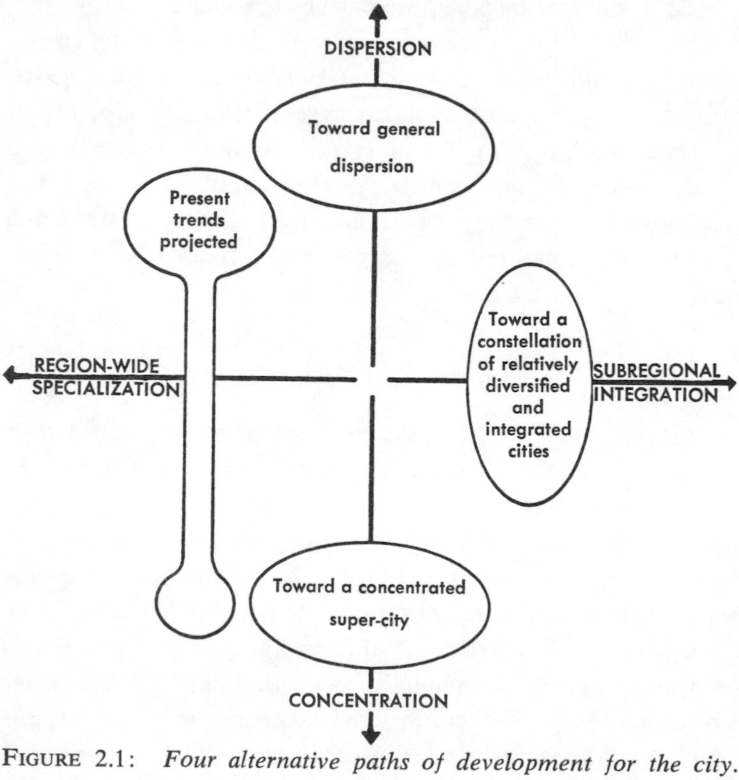

FIGURE 2.1: *Four alternative paths of development for the city.*

possible. Thus, conflicts between the old pattern and new directions have to be resolved gradually along the way, with considerable flexibility.

With these qualifications Figure 2.1 indicates roughly how several alternatives might relate to the two coordinates:

1. *Present trends projected.* Region-wide specialization with most functions dispersed but with a push toward greater concentration of certain functions in the central cities. Perhaps unstable, likely to shift toward one of the other alternatives.

2. *General dispersion.* Probably toward region-wide specialization of certain functions but a considerable degree of subregional integration might be induced.

3. *Concentrated super-city.* Probably with a strong tendency toward specialized sectors for different functions.

4. *Constellation of relatively diversified and integrated cities.* With cities of differing size and character a range from moderate dispersion to moderate concentration would be feasible.

Terms for Comparison: Ends and Means

Differences in urban form and structure must be evaluated in terms of the set of human ends (or benefits) they will serve, the other ends forgone, and the differing means (or costs) required to achieve these benefits. Each of our alternatives is a package of goods favoring a particular set of values and life-styles and having a particular price tag attached. But it is a hypothetical package, and in the present primitive state of urban cost-benefit analysis it is impossible to know exactly what the goods are, or what we would have to pay for them.

The ends can be compared in relatively simple, concrete terms, such as housing choice, job accessibility, class and race patterns. But the deeper social and economic effects will be harder to assess: productive efficiency and individual opportunity; family welfare, privacy, security, and cosmopolitan stimulation; quality of communications, adaptability to further change, social relations, and responsible citizenship. In a period when social science is mainly telling us how little we really know about needs and tastes, perhaps the range of environmental choice afforded by a particular urban pattern may be a factor of major importance. And this may be especially true of the residential environment, which offers very limited choices to most households today.

But the desirability of a particular package also depends on the means required to achieve it. Appropriate cost comparisons include the private and public expenditures for major items such as housing, transportation, redevelopment, and open space; the forms and degrees of public power that must be exercised at various levels of government; and broad social costs such as enforced dislocation, destruction of existing values, and waste of resources. In an extremely rough and general way, some of these differentials may be fairly obvious, while others are impossible to evaluate.

These are complex questions in a pioneering field, and all I can provide are some tentative and undoubtedly biased judgments. If they provoke debate and more systematic analysis, they will have fully served their purpose.

Trends, Countertrends, and the Potential for Change

Planning, in Perloff's and Wingo's words, must be related to "the things that matter: the major social movements." I have tried to identify some of "the things that matter" which have a direct influence on urban form and structure because they are the forces behind certain key trends and variables. Two dimensions have been selected: from extreme dispersion (low density and scatteration) to extreme concentration (high density, contiguity, and strong centering); and from large-scale integration (a single metropolitan system with specialized parts) to small-scale subintegration (diversified communities within the region with relatively balanced facilities for most ordinary functions). In these terms, what are the significant current trends and the forces behind them? What are the resulting problems and conflicts which could change the present picture?

Centrifugal Forces: The Selective Push for Private Space

The dominant trend toward low densities and scatteration in out-lying development reflects the demand for private space for certain functions: large areas to permit greater freedom on the site for industrial production and building operations, for shops and schools, and above all for middle- and upper-class family life. Closely related to the latter is the desire for natural amenity at home in private gardens and attractive vistas (and also increasingly in vacation cabins which produce a much wider ring of scattered development). Land speculation enhances the trend but is not the prime cause. In addition to these outward pulls, there is also the push to escape from city conditions—obsolete housing or inadequate schools, racial and cultural diversity, conflict, discomfort, high taxes, and helplessness—into small, safe, homogeneous, self-run communities with middle-class standards and status.

These varied "private" purposes which are related to the qualities of a particular site or small neighborhood area have been brought within reach by the achievement of another kind of private value, *automobility,* which permits individual freedom of circulation in a piece of personal property. Because private autos perform badly in the traditional type of multipurpose urban center, automobility has also contributed to the dispersal of business, cultural, and service facilities. Technology is serving these ends in other ways too: new equipment makes both houses and factories more self-sufficient; large-scale building operations provide most of their own utilities for standardized one-price homes; and rising opportunities for long-distance communications—mail, phone, radio, TV, and travel—make the individual or firm less dependent on immediate physical contacts within the metropolitan area.

These choices are open today, however, only to limited groups and functions: relatively foot-loose industries and businesses; the services that follow resident populations; families able to acquire suburban homes despite high prices, restrictive zoning practices, race discrimination, and rising taxes.

Of course, there is a great deal of medium- and high-density development, old and new. But dispersal has been the dominant trend for several decades, reflecting the conscious choice of multitudes of consumers and entrepreneurs. It has produced unanticipated problems and generated some counterforces, but unless these actually weaken the basic drives for private space they will probably not have much effect. In these terms, is the push for dispersal likely to increase or decline in the future?

The desired life style of most American families with children still seems to call for the private home with a yard. High marriage and birth rates, and upward mobility with rising incomes and education, will only increase this demand, as will any abatement in race discrimination, or policies to provide cheaper housing in outlying areas.

There are, however, some qualifying factors in the trend toward endless suburban sprawl. Rising land prices and the demand for a wider range of dwelling types to suit varied household types and tastes are producing a greater admixture of multifamily rental units in some localities. Large-scale operations tend to result in patches of contiguous development, sometimes at "city" scale and including rental housing, community facilities, and industry. Public awareness of the costs of scatteration is likewise mounting, due to high taxes for inadequate services on the one hand, and the rising demand to preserve public open space and natural amenity within metropolitan areas, on the other. But measures to insure more compact development, or open space reservation, are not yet generally effective.

The force of purely "escape" motivations can become either stronger or weaker, depending largely on the increase or decline of race and class prejudice for whatever reasons, and the degree to which older cities become more or less ghettoized, or suburbia more mixed.

Accessibility to work is also an ambivalent factor. The business and professional people who continue to work in central cities have been willing to pay a high price for their home environment, in transportation time, trouble, and expense. But as their journey to work increases, or requires both a private car and one or more public conveyances, other solutions may be sought. If the offices move out to accommodate them, this can mean more dispersal. But if they settle for higher density housing, whether in the city or near a mass transit stop, it would have the opposite effect. Similarly, the factories and services which depend on relatively low-paid labor cannot move very far away from the old central districts, so long as the supply of cheap housing is predominantly located there. But if the suburban housing market were broadened, these jobs might become more dispersed.

The number of second homes for leisure-time use will probably increase enormously. This will broaden the extent of scatteration throughout a vast region, but at the same time it might conceivably mean greater acceptance of compact development, with greater convenience to work and other urban facilities, for weekday use.

In any case, centrifugal forces and private values, however dominant in new development, are still countered by some opposing influences, actual or potential.

Centripetal Forces: By Choice and By Compulsion

The revival of skyscraper office development in many downtown districts reflects the continued demand among certain types of business enterprise for face-to-face contacts and adjacent services within "walking precincts," or merely for the prestige value of a particular location. This is clearly a conscious choice, despite the increased ease of long-distance communication and the increased burden of commuting; and it is therefore a centralizing factor which is likely to endure in some form. However, routine or mechanical office operations are beginning to move out, along with industry and consumer services. Over-all employment is unlikely to increase in most central cities, and business districts may tend to become specialized enclaves, whether they stay downtown or move outside.

In most cities, the old consumer uses of the center for shopping, amusement, and cultural pursuits have either remained static or declined, despite metropolitan growth. Where entertainment does thrive, it seems to owe its existence primarily to "visiting firemen," business travelers, vacationers, and conventiongoers rather than the local suburbanites who, as a matter of fact, may be more likely to patronize a central theatre or restaurant when visiting in some other city.

In general the choice of central locations for business and leisure use still appears to be strongest in cities with traditionally strong centers, like New York and San Francisco, and weakest in cities which have always been more or less dispersed, such as Detroit and Los Angeles.

The other major use of central cities is both more universal and much more involuntary: lower-income and minority households are forced to concentrate there, by and large, because old districts provide the only major source of cheap or unrestricted housing—whether in obsolete structures or new subsidized projects, and regardless of locational trends in their particular job opportunities. If the rate of upward mobility increases, or if the flow of disadvantaged in-migrants finally begins to dry up, or if the suburban housing market is expanded, this part of the picture might change quite rapidly. The degree to which they would choose suburban living, if they could, is sometimes questioned. The crowded slum enclave offers a semblance of security to the recent arrival and the disadvantaged, . . . as redevelopers have belatedly discovered. But all our urban history suggests that their aspirations are probably not very different from those of the millions who have moved upward and outward before them.

Some middle- and upper-income white people have stayed in the cities by choice, of course, but increasingly these have been single workers, adult households, Bohemians, and—if the attractions are great enough—wealthy families who put their children in private schools and have second homes in the country.

Those who voluntarily select a tight city environment for homes or business have something in common. They all value private space and the freedom of automobility far less than the attractions of convenience to work, the opportunity for specialized contacts and facilities within a small area, the stimulation of diversity, or the sense of being part of a cosmopolitan community in direct touch with world affairs. These are traditional urban values, and it is quite possible that more would choose them if they could be had without a heavy sacrifice in private living conditions. Yet, the half-worlds of City-and-Suburb rarely offer such a choice.

This is the background situation, but there is a rising push to "save" the central cities which is taking two positive forms: urban renewal programs with federal aid, and efforts to create or improve mass transit systems for commuting. These movements stem primarily from the increasingly desperate desire of economic and political interests in the central cities to protect property values and the tax base, with a variable intermingling of other forces, such as the need to provide better housing for slum-dwellers and the new wave of intellectual concern for urban historical and cultural values, which also tends to be anti-suburbia and anti-automobile.

Redevelopment brings new private and public structures of various types—office buildings and apartments, civic and cultural facilities—usually at increased densities and all subsidized to varying degrees. Expensive apartments predominate, but there are also middle-income ventures and low-rent public housing projects. In addition (often in opposition) conservationist programs are active here and there.

Central city traffic conditions have been worsened by the tremendous expenditures in freeway construction since the war, and it is now widely recognized that large-scale concentration is incompatible with universal dependence on private automobility.

Despite the declining use of public transportation, the improvement or creation of metropolitan transit systems is a lively issue with several entirely new schemes either built, approved, or under discussion.

To the extent that these movements fulfill their present aims they will tend to maintain or promote concentration, at least for certain types of residence, work, and leisure-time activity. But these programs are very expensive, in terms of both financial subsidy and such disruptive social costs as forcible dislocation, and the degree to which they can actually offset the predominant trend toward dispersal depends on many imponderables. Will the restrictions of the housing market continue to force most low-income and minority households to live in the old cities, whether in successive blighted areas or in heavily subsidized public housing projects? Will the Negroes use their rising political power for greater integration throughout the metropolitan area or for separatist strength within the central cities? To what extent will middle-class white families and business enterprise favor convenience and city attractions if it means political domination by lower-income and minority voters? Will mass transit mainly facilitate more two-way commuting, instead of more jobs in the city?

The movement to save old cities has been narrowly focused on central problems thus far, with little concern for the pattern of outlying development or the desirable form and structure of the region as a whole. This may change. It is already recognized that transportation is a region-wide problem in its political as well as in its functional aspects. Regional population distribution is likely to become a mounting issue, in terms of housing choice, suburban race and class discrimination, the increasing disparity between residence and job opportunities, and, above all, the tendency of central cities to become ghettoized with all the related implications for tax-base problems and renewal hopes.

These issues are just beginning to be posed, however. Effective measures to deal with the shape and structure of regional development have not yet been devised, and no public image of the appropriate goals has developed. Housing, land use, transportation and renewal policies could be used not only to promote either dispersion or concentration, but also to encourage a wider range of residential choice in both outlying and central areas. This leads into the whole question of "balance" and the level of functional and political integration, which is the second dimension I wish to discuss.

Toward Region-Wide Specialization: A Single Super-City?

The widespread dispersal of certain functions, while others remain highly concentrated, generates a pattern which poses some basic structural issues. In a way it is still the classic form of the modern city, with business in the center, industry on the fringe, and the outward neighborhood succession from poor to rich, only greatly expanded in all its dimensions and administered by hundreds of independent local governments. At the moderate scale of a single municipality, the urban community had problems of slums and services, but the pattern itself posed no great difficulties. For the metropolitan complex, however, communications and integration are critical issues which raise questions about social, economic, and political structure.

Above the neighborhood level with its domestic functions, is the metropolis necessarily a single organic system with highly differentiated parts? Is it essentially one labor and job market, one housing market, one set of leisure-time and service facilities? Is it made up of so many specialized but interdependent activity orbits of varying scale that they can only be integrated at the metropolitan level? If this is true, then the basic problems are likely to be intercommunications and unified regional government.

Or can it be too big to operate sensibly or efficiently as a single system? Could the ordinary activities of the vast majority of people be better cared for within subregional sectors or smaller diversified communities? If so, then basic changes in housing and land use policy are required within a structure of stronger local governments co-operating through some kind of regional federation. There are influences in both directions, and the picture presented here is inevitably over-simplified, but the strongest current trends seem to lean toward specialized sectors and communities rather than subregional integration, with central cities and outlying areas serving quite different but highly interdependent functions. Consider the distribution of resident population, jobs, and leisure-time facilities with some of the resulting disparities.

The social divisions among residents of old cities and newer suburbs are increasingly sharp, by income level, by age group, and, above all, by race. These divisions are largely created by the housing pattern, and strengthened by the limitations of the current housing market, which by and large serves only upper and upper-middle income white families in areas of recent growth. If present trends continue, low-income and minority households will soon predominate in many central cities.

Meanwhile, the locational specialization of employment and business enterprise is following a different pattern, with most new industrial and service jobs outside the cities, and certain types of office and professional work still downtown. As for outdoor recreation, any major open spaces that may yet be saved are likely to be out beyond the fringe, near people who already have private land but far away from the families who live in crowded slums or high-rise projects and who frequently do not have automobiles. For urban leisure-time activities, the old multipurpose centers provide cheap attractions for the poor, and also, to varying degrees, Bohemia for the beatniks and intellectuals, and very expensive entertainment for the rich and the visiting firemen. Equivalent middle-class facilities are likely to be scattered around outside or in specialized suburban "centers" for shopping, culture, or amusement (Disneyland, for example).

This pattern poses obvious problems of extended cross-commuting, of limited housing choice, of accessibility to an adequate choice of leisure-time facilities, and of critical tax-base discrepancies. It is a serious threat to the future of current renewal efforts. These problems may be the inevitable price of the increasing specialization which produced great urban agglomerations in the first place, and their solution may require a strong metropolitan government to insure over-all productive efficiency, equity, and effectiveness of intercommunication. The inherent trends, however, confront us with a paradox: the sharpening class and race divisions along with the tax-base disparities lead to deepening political conflict between central cities and suburbia which makes metropolitan unification ever more difficult, if not impossible, unless it is imposed by direct state or federal intervention.

The Potential for Subregional Integration

The American metropolis has in certain ways been moving toward a vast unitary "city"-type structure with highly specialized interdependent parts, and it cannot be claimed that there is any conscious countermovement to encourage a greater degree of functional balance and self-containment within subregional sectors. Proposals for "satellite communities" keep coming up in metropolitan plans, however, doubtless stimulated by the evidence from Britain and elsewhere that relatively independent new towns can be developed successfully, while renewal programs reflect efforts to create in central areas a better balanced population related to downtown employment opportunities. But the relation of the functional structure of metropolitan areas to the development pattern has received inadequate research attention; we have little practical understanding of how it works now or how its workings might be improved. Obviously it is an overlay of numerous interlocking activity patterns, large and small, including many that extend far beyond the region, and many that are normally circumscribed within a neighborhood. But we do not really know to what degree and for what specific purposes the entire region is necessarily a single system. In question particularly are certain functions which used to be integrated at the city-wide level, such as the special consumer demands which brought people to central districts, and above all the trip between home and work. It is frequently assumed that these activities, with their implied range of choices, can only be encompassed to any significant degree today at the metropolitan-wide scale. But there are trends and pressures which tend to favor some form of subregional integration.

Human activity systems range all the way from the bedroom-bathroom trek to the astronaut's orbit around the moon. Within the metropolitan complex, a great many functions have catchment areas which are normally quite limited: schools, playgrounds, meeting-halls, churches, ordinary shops, services and amusements, even junior colleges, general hospitals, super shopping centers, and little theatres.

The pattern varies tremendously with personal means and tastes. Some people go to any lengths to visit a race track, a symphony concert, an exotic restaurant, or a wilderness park, which others would ignore if they were next door. In between, a growing number of people would enjoy such specialties if they were fairly accessible. By the same token, many of the special "goods" can and should be more numerous and more accessible—in theory at least—because it would take a smaller over-all population to provide the selective demand. Mumford's principle of the cultural "grid," based on the British Museum's decentralized library service, is important for some of the highly refined but mobile resources. And if a tight multipurpose center has the stimulating and universal advantages claimed for it by central city saviors, then a large metropolitan region should probably have several such centers to serve the potential demand.

The critical questions seem to stem from the relations between the spatial systems of residence and employment. We have been acquiring some information about commuting patterns, and there will be more . . . , but intensive analysis is also needed: case histories for a sampling of different occupations in different areas, including employment changes, residential changes, and how both jobs and homes were found. From preliminary Census data on commuting patterns as well as from more intensive recent studies it appears that the number of employed people who somehow manage to live and work in the same subregional sector may be surprisingly high, considering the limitations of choice in the housing market. Both home-moves and job-moves within a metropolitan area appear to be frequently influenced by a desire to reduce the journey-to-work, even at the cost of breaking family ties or living in a less desirable home on the one hand, or subordinating economic opportunity to home values on the other. People who make such choices do not see or use the whole region as a single urban community: many of its opportunities might as well be in another area entirely. The lack of convenient jobs may therefore promote residential mobility, neighborhood instability and long-distance commuting, while the restrictions on housing choice can tend to limit economic opportunity, particularly for low-income and minority households. Of course, accessibility is more important than mapped distances, and my rather conservative judgments must be balanced against Webber's revolutionary concepts of metropolitan communications potentials. But it seems fairly clear that technology has not yet overcome the friction of space for the metropolitan commuter.

Although the residential pattern is greatly influenced by public actions, these broad locational issues have not yet been seriously posed in American planning or policy. The suburban market for new housing is limited more than ever to upper-income white families, while federal aids for low-cost housing are confined to city renewal and rehousing programs. Most European countries, however, have long assumed that new housing development must accommodate a more or less cross-section population. In the United States strong pressures are building up against suburban racial barriers and for a wider range of housing choice for middle- and lower-income families of all races and household types. The central cities may come to support these pressures, although their political motivations will be mixed. But both state and federal governments will be increasingly involved in the rising metropolitan issues of class and race, of city and suburbs, of tax inequities, transportation costs, and general inefficiency.

Present trends might shift, therefore, toward a somewhat wider balance of population in both outlying areas and the central city, posing the possibility of greater functional integration below the metropolitan level. Strong resistance from existing suburban communities will affect the resulting pattern, however. Will there be a scattering of additional types of one-class enclave, for middle-class Negroes, for the aged, for cheaper homes? Can the present suburban communities, many of which already have industries, be induced to become socially diversified? Will entirely new cities be developed on the remote fringe where a wide range of housing and job choices may be particularly desirable? Can a reasonably healthy social balance be maintained in the central cities?

Alternative Directions for Form and Structure: Some Rough Comparisons

The wide range of hypothetical possibility seems to come down to four reasonably practicable alternatives. The dominance of one or the other in a particular situation would depend on the dominant public, private, and individual purposes behind the environment-shaping decisions, the acceptibility of the means required to achieve certain purposes, and differing local conditions which might enhance or impede the feasibility of moving in certain directions.

Before considering these alternatives and their implications in more concrete terms, let us try to summarize the conceivable public attitudes that would lead in one direction or another—the various common images of the future metropolis that might be influential. At the same time, certain precedents and prototypes which relate to these different sets of attitudes will be suggested, including Utopian images and practical experience.

Common Images and Their Prototypes

1. "There's nothing serious that can't be solved by better transportation and central improvements." Seen from this viewpoint, quite prevalent among business and political leaders, it seems that some of the experts are making too much fuss.

There's nothing abnormal or seriously wrong about the present metropolitan pattern, they feel. A lot of people like suburban living, and it's fine if they can afford it. The others must naturally live in older districts, but they will gradually move outward into better dwellings as we tear down the worst to make way for new apartments and office buildings. If necessary we can build some public housing. Of course, the metropolitan area is essentially a single community, and there should really be some kind of overall government and planning, but local vested interests may be too strong. However, the state and federal governments can help to equalize the tax burdens a bit, to save some open space, and above all to solve the transportation problem. As long as we can get around, whether by automobile or mass transit or both, we'll be all right.

Since this simply assumes the projection of present trends which are visible in most American metropolitan areas, no additional illustrations or prototypes are necessary.

2. "Let people have what they want: space and mobility." This attitude, very unfashionable in intellectual and downtown business or government circles today, reflects such powerful popular forces, however inarticulate, that it might win out. The rationale behind it might be put into words as follows: It is stupid and reactionary to put huge public investments into central redevelopment and mass transit. People don't want to live or travel that way any more, and they won't unless they're forced to. Open up plenty of new land and build plenty of homes on it for all kinds and classes. Even if some of it were subsidized it would be a lot cheaper than current redevelopment and public housing projects. And it would offer the slum dwellers a real choice which many of them would be glad to accept, instead of merely forcing them out of their present homes into something no better. More and more jobs will follow the people, and perhaps commuting could get easier. When the old city is thinned out, it will be simpler and cheaper to fix it up for the few things that really need to be there, which people can then reach by car. Most of the old-time city attractions are better outside where they have more space.

These are the forces that shaped Los Angeles and stimulate its fantastic growth despite the smog and other problems. At the Utopian level, the same values are reflected in Frank Lloyd Wright's "Broadacre City," and in Buckminster Fuller's lifelong effort to develop a completely mobile and self-contained house, free of the utility network. In some ways Melvin Webber's theoretical emphasis on the spatial freedom resulting from communications technology leads to a similar viewpoint.

3. "The Metropolis is a single Great City: pull it together and urbanize it." This is the fashionable sophisticated view among the new urbanists, including many critical writers, social scientists, modern architects, central renewal promoters, and certain economic interests. The number of conscious adherents is probably quite small, but the intellectuals have often turned out to be the vanguard of much larger movements, and the potential strength of this view should not be discounted. It has various facets which are oversimplified and perhaps exaggerated in this brief interpretation: Great concentrated cosmopolitan cities, with their close contacts and stimulating diversity, have always been the source of civilization. The metropolitan community is still essentially a city, no matter how many people there are in it, but it is being disintegrated by the boring sprawl and stupid escapism of suburbia and the automobile. City and country are two entirely different things, while the suburban hybrid has the virtues of neither one nor the other and is rapidly destroying both. We should put a stop to all scattered fringe development, fill in suburbia with apartment houses, greatly densify and diversify the old center (although some would like to save its historic flavor), develop the best possible mass transit system, forbid private cars in cities wherever possible, and in general promote an exciting and civilized life. Week-ends, if we want a change, we can go to real country or the wilderness. Nearby open spaces for everyday recreational use can also be saved, if we stop suburban scatteration in time.

Utopias related to this view range from the technocratic models of Le Corbusier and the Bauhaus leaders to the nostalgic humanism of Jane Jacobs. It is also reflected in official planning practices, inevitably somewhat modified, in many central city renewal programs (with no suburban jurisdiction however), and in metropolitan planning for Philadelphia, Copenhagen, and (mixed with the fourth alternative) Stockholm.

4. "The behemoth is too big to be a single city: guide growth, at least, into relatively self-contained communities." This is an old reform movement which has had many followers and widespread international influence in various guises. Rather scorned by the current *avant-garde*, it is quite as much an urbanist, anti-sprawl philosophy as it is anti-Big-City, and still has considerable appeal to a large and varied group of people, roughly in the following terms:

Instead of scattering houses, factories, shops, offices and services all over the landscape, we should pull them together into compact cities, with adjacent open space saved for recreation, agriculture and general amenity. There would be disagreement as to ideal city size, but suitable housing for a cross-section population should be provided, with more emphasis on row houses and garden apartments. A variety of employment opportunities should be encouraged, as well as a bona fide urban center. The cities would be readily accessible to each other and to the central city; indeed, such a pattern would favor a mass transit system if it is needed. The central city would normally provide certain region-wide services, and its population should also become better balanced. Some kind of regional federation and effective regional planning would be necessary. But local government would in many ways be strengthened, and democratic citizenship made more meaningful. A balanced choice of city and nature, privacy and opportunity, would be available to everyone.

These principles were originally stimulated by the Garden City movement, which led directly to the postwar British program of New Towns and expanded old towns. But they also have much broader manifestations: the current reorganization of Greater London into moderate-sized districts with considerable powers of self-government; Israel with its carefully developed state-wide system of cities and towns; the great metropolitan circle of old and new cities in Holland with the center reserved for agriculture and recreation; Stockholm's arc of satellites within the city limits; and various planning efforts in the United States, including the Year 2000 scheme for the National Capital Region and some California proposals.

Four Alternatives

How would these variant directions tend to work out? Would they fulfill the claims made by their proponents? What local conditions would favor one or the other? Following are some brief personal judgments:

1. Present trends projected. The wider dispersal of certain special classes and functions into outlying areas, with greater concentration of others in central districts, would probably tend to magnify the present problems of accessibility, inadequate choice, social and political schisms, and rising costs, particularly for transportation and housing. This might therefore be an unstable pattern, likely to push eventually toward one of the other alternatives, and there would in any case be an increasing degree of intervention by state and federal governments. The ultimate direction taken in a particular locality would depend in part on present limitations and opportunities in the area, in part on locally determined goals and actions, and in part on federal and state inducements.

2. Toward general dispersion. The underlying popular forces which favor low-density scattered development, particularly the desire for private space and automobility, are still very strong. If they become increasingly dominant, more housing for lower-income and minority househoulds will be made available in outlying areas, with federal and state assistance in new forms. This will hasten the decentralization of industry and even the most specialized consumer services. Some office functions may try to remain downtown where they are now highly centralized, and it would be easier to provide acceptable housing for middle-income and upper-income families in the old centers as they are thinned out and become less dominated by lower-class population. But the expanse of the region would be so enormous in the larger metropolitan areas that even the region-wide functions might tend to be scattered around, in some cases in close but highly specialized groups.

There could be a tendency for homes and work opportunities to be somewhat closer than they would be if present trends were projected. But subregional integration in any clearcut form is highly unlikely. Instead there would be a complex chain-like system of overlapping catchment areas for daily activities, extending outward indefinitely, as is already more or less visible in southern California. Residential development would probably continue to take the form of socially specialized enclaves, and class and race conflicts would make the creation of large suburban cities even more difficult than it is today. Service costs would be high, due to scatteration. Because there would be no strong reason for new development to be close to existing development, public open spaces and agriculture could be preserved, but this would call for direct state action. Indeed, all the unified powers required to maintain service and communications networks, and equalize tax burdens, would probably have to be exercised by state and federal agencies, either directly or through the creation of a regional government by their initiative.

Some will argue, with Webber, that increasing accessibility plus aspatial communication overcomes distance, with the result that people living at exurban densities can participate effectively in numerous realms, including a strong local community, and enjoy urban values along with their private space and mobility. This is a real issue, worthy of the most intensive study, but I am yet to be convinced. In my perhaps conservative and rather anti-technocratic view, the argument holds up for most of the personally selective and specialized realms of communication and interaction, and of course for one-way mass communication by TV and such, but not for the kind of community which provides contacts and responsibilities that cut across special interests creating common ground and stimulating mutual adjustment and integration. And I suspect that specialization, without an effective framework for integration, may be the basic curse and threat of our times, whether at the local, national, or international level.

In our social, civic, and political life we have not learned how to apply the real lesson of the scientific and industrial revolution: the cross-communication and interdependence that make specialization effective in the common interest.

This pattern is hardly possible in regions with highly concentrated populations where metropolitan areas are already beginning to overlap, such as the central section of the Atlantic Coast. To accommodate future growth they will be forced to choose one of the other alternatives. To the extent that these values have universal force, however, the rate of westward migration is likely to be stimulated. On the other hand, the people who have moved to the West are already somewhat self-selected to favor a dispersed pattern of living.

3. Toward a concentrated super-city. This is probably the least likely alternative, except under very special conditions. But if we are at the start of a general swing toward a Manhattan life-style, with supporting policies at all levels of government, programs for high-density redevelopment in central cities will be greatly accelerated for all income groups and for a variety of functions. State and federal action would prevent further sprawl in outlying areas, and a powerful metropolitan government would fill in the scattered spaces between present suburbs (often with industrial development) and rezone them for multiple dwellings. The most advanced technology would be applied to mass transit and high-rise structures, perhaps with coordinated three-dimensional circulation in central districts. Private automobiles would be banned wherever possible, and pedestrian enclaves encouraged.

This pattern would tend, I think, toward a high degree of functional and social specialization in its various sectors. Structures and subareas would have to be carefully designed to fit particular activities, and social conflicts among heterogeneous populations could be aggravated if they were mixed up together in such close quarters.

One problem will be difficult to solve: the enormous demand for week-end homes in secluded locations, with attractive natural surroundings. Perhaps this could be managed by providing air or rail service to many distant centers where family station-wagons would be kept.

Costs would be very high for central reconstruction and transportation, and would be increased by the demand for second homes with automobiles for recreational purposes.

The New York region particularly might tend in this direction because it has limited space, a highly centralized power structure, and a population that is probably more or less self-selected to favor these values.

4. Toward a constellation of relatively diversified and intengrated cities. If the desire for private space and natural amenity is modified by greater concern for accessibility, diversity, and other traditional urban values, a tendency toward subregional integration could take various forms. Housing for all classes, races, and age-groups would, in any case, be provided in new outlying development, at mixed densities, and related to varied employment opportunities in the same general area. Since these cities would be fairly self-contained, they could be located quite far out on cheap land. This would require strong public and private initiative combined in some new form of agency. It could also be done by stimulating more balanced development in suburban communities already started, but this would encounter considerable resistance and require very ingenious inducements not yet devised. A system of greenbelts or wedges could be preserved, but this would require state or federal initiative at the start, when it would be most needed, pending the formation of a regional federation of cities with the necessary powers.

The transportation system would be subject to the same conditions. It could either be predominantly by rail (if larger, denser cities are favored) or by automobile for relatively small, low-density communities. Mass transit would not be as necessary for commuting as it is now, and distant intercity communications could conceivably be handled by air.

The old central city might remain quite strong, for region-wide functions and highly specialized facilities, but it would have less employment and a relatively balanced population with mixed densities and dwelling types. There would be far less disruption and dislocation than in the Super-City alternative with a much greater chance to preserve the diversity and historic qualities which make for real "urbanity." Where dominant central cities do not now exist, there might be a tendency for the specialized regional functions to settle in various cities (Clarence Stein's model), strengthening their centers and differentiating their region-wide attractions. In general, the cities might vary greatly in size and character, and they could either become a fairly close-knit regional network with minimal space between or spread quite far out into a larger region, depending on variable purposes and conditions. For those who prefer them, there could be homogenous, but only partly self-governing, enclaves. Except for the extremes of scatteration, concentration, and specialization, this pattern would probably offer the greatest choice in life-styles.

Costs would be relatively low, compared with any of the other alternatives, due to less scatteration on the one hand, and less high-density construction on the other. If rail mass transit is provided in addition to automobile circulation, this would add to costs but strengthen centers. Property values in the old central cities would have to be written down to some degree, but on the other hand, land for new development and big parks could be quite cheap if it were acquired in time.

In one form or another, this alternative would be feasible in almost any metropolitan area. It calls for no greater exercise of public power than is now applied to redevelopment, but basic innovations in policy and purpose would be required.

These are very sketchy and personal judgments as to the nature of the alternatives, the forces behind them, and their comparative significance. I would only argue that this *kind* of approach is needed to make both the science and art of environmental planning effective. Within a framework which poses a range of hypotheses as to the future form and structure of the urban complex, our pioneering efforts toward systematic understanding of the development process should be applied to the analysis of ends and means, and the weighing of costs and benefits, in particular situations. The same framework can, I think, enhance the art of public communication, which is a major responsibility of both planner and researcher. With creative imagination based on scientific analysis, the big choices open to public decision can be clearly presented.

3 *The Urban Field*

JOHN FRIEDMANN
JOHN MILLER

John Friedmann and John Miller, city planners now at the University of California, Los Angeles, and the Massachusetts Institute of Technology, distinguish between metropolitan areas and the intermetropolitan periphery, that area outside and between the metropolitan areas. As the urban scale expands and penetrates into the declining intermetropolitan periphery, a new urban unit will emerge, the urban field. *This unit will include the core metropolitan area and the surrounding intermetropolitan periphery perhaps two hours drive (roughly one hundred miles) from the center. If appropriately planned for, this emerging pattern will encourage new life styles that will allow for "a wider life space," greater choice among alternative "living environments," and a "wider community of interests."*

There has been a growing dissatisfaction with the historical concept of the city. Don Martindale, in his brilliant introduction to Max Weber's essay, *The City,* has composed a fitting epitaph:

> The modern city is losing its external and formal structure. Internally it is in a state of decay while the new community represented by the nation everywhere grows at its expense. The age of the city seems to be at an end.[1]

If this is so from a sociological standpoint, it is equally true from the perspective of a physical planner. Various concepts have been put forward in the endeavor to capture the expanding

Reprinted by permission of the authors and the *Journal of the American Institute of Planners,* Vol. 21, No. 4 (November, 1965), pp. 312–20.

scale of urban life. Metropolitan region, spread city, megalopolis, ecumenopolis . . . each attempt to redefine the new reality has led to a broader spatial conception. Behind these efforts lies an awareness of the constantly widening patterns of interaction in an urbanizing world.

Modern utopian constructs have been equally intent on fitting city concepts to the possibilities created by our communications-based society. Clarence Stein's *Regional City* is a constellation of moderately sized communities separated by great open spaces and bound closely together by highways.[2] Frank Lloyd Wright's *Broadacre City* represents a complete melting of the urban and rural worlds that, without pronounced centers, would uniformly dissolve throughout a region.[3] Both these constructs see the city as an essentially unlimited form of human settlement, capable of infinite expansion.

None of the new concepts, however, has been completely successful. The Bureau of the Census has had to shift the meaning of metropolitan region from "metropolitan district" to "standard metropolitan area" to "standard metropolitan statistical area" in order to keep pace with our improved understanding of what constitutes the fundamental ecological area of urban life, and it is once more reexamining the question.[4]

The much looser conception of *spread-city* has been applied only to the New York region, and no attempt has been made to generalize from it to other urban areas.[5] Jean Gottman's *megalopolis* appears as a geographic place name for the chain of metropolitan giants along the Boston-Washington axis.[6] Although later writers have taken it as a generic term for contiguous metropolitan regions, the concept, lacking precision as well as generality, has frequently been misapplied. One writer has gone so far as to extend its meaning to the entire region from Phoenix to Minneapolis.[7] His Midwest Central Megalopolis is a geographic and conceptual absurdity. Finally, C. A. Doxiadis' *ecumenopolis* is no concept at all but a poetic vision.[8]

Planners therefore, are left in a quandary. "Modern metropolitan trends," wrote the late Catherine Bauer Wurster, "have destroyed the traditional concept of urban structure, and there is no new image to take its place."[9] Yet none would question the need for such an image, if only to serve as the conceptual basis for organizing our strategies for urban development. Our hope in this paper is to meet this great need, suggesting an image of the new *polis* that will be adequate to the tasks that face the nation in the decades ahead.

THE ENLARGED SCALE OF URBAN LIFE

It has become increasingly possible to interpret the spatial structure of the United States in ways that will emphasize a pattern consisting of *one,* metropolitan areas and *two,* the intermetropolitan periphery. Except for thinly populated parts of the American interior, the intermetropolitan periphery includes all areas that intervene among metropolitan regions that are, as it were, the reverse image of the trend towards large scale concentrated settlement that has persisted in this country for over half a century. Like a devil's mirror, much of it has developed a socioeconomic profile that perversely reflects the very opposite of metropolitan virility.

Economically, the intermetropolitan periphery includes most of the areas that have been declared eligible for federal area redevelopment assistance.[10] . . . [These areas] have a disproportionately large share of low-growth and declining industries and a correspondingly antiquated economic structure. Nevertheless, one-fifth of the American people are living in these regions of economic distress.

Demographically, the intermetropolitan periphery has been subject to a long-term, continuous decline. This trend reflects the movement of people to cities, especially to the large metropolitan concentrations. Although the smaller cities on the periphery have to some extent benefitted from mitration, their gains have been less, on the average, than for all urban areas.[11] In addition, migration from economically depressed regions has been highly selective, so that the age distribution of the remaining population has become polarized around the very young and very old. In

Appalachia, for example, the two million people who left the region during the 1950s were, for the most part, drawn from the productive age groups from 18 to 64. At the same time, the population over 65 years old increased by nearly one-third.[12] In some areas, recorded death rates now actually exceed birth rates.[13]

Socially, the standard indices of education and health are substantially lower along the periphery than in metropolitan areas. The quality of public services has deteriorated (though their *per capita* cost has increased), the housing stock is older, and the level of educational attainment is significantly below the average for metropolitan America. Rapid and selective outmigration, a declining economic base, the burden of an aging population, and low incomes have rendered many peripheral communities helpless in their desire to adapt to changing circumstances in the outside world. The remaining population is frequently short both on civic leadership and hope. They can neither grasp the scope of the events that have overtaken them nor are they capable of responding creatively to the new situations.[14]

Politically, many peripheral areas have lost their ability to act. They are fragmented, disorganized, and without effective economic leverage. The Area Redevelopment Administration has for a number of years been at work in these regions on a county by county basis (itself a fragmented strategy) and now the Appalachia program has been launched amidst much fanfare. Yet neither of these programs has adequately recognized the relationship between metropolitan cores and their peripheries, so their scale, though ambitious, has been dwarfed by the extent of the social and economic problems of the periphery.

The emergence in large sections of the country of the intermetropolitan periphery as a major problem area has been the direct result of the concentration of people and activities around closely contiguous metropolitan cores. Growth in and around these cores has drawn off the productive population, economic activities, and investment capital of the periphery, but the forces of urbanization are now in the process of reversing this trend.[15]

Looking ahead to the next generation, we foresee a new scale of urban living that will extend far beyond existing metropolitan cores and penetrate deeply into the periphery. Relations of dominance and dependency will be transcended. The older established centers, together with the intermetropolitan peripheries that envelop them, will constitute the new ecological unit of America's postindustrial society that will replace traditional concepts of the city and metropolis. This basic element of the emerging spatial order we shall call the *urban field.*

The urban field may be viewed as an enlargement of the space for urban living that extends far beyond the boundaries of existing metropolitan areas—defined primarily in terms of commuting to a central city of "metropolitan" size—into the open landscape of the periphery. This change to a larger scale of urban life is already underway, encouraged by changes in technology, economics, and preferred social behavior. Eventually the urban field may even come to be acknowledged as a community of *shared* interests, although these interests may be more strongly oriented to specific functions than to area. They will be shared because to a large extent they will overlap and complement each other within a specific locational matrix. Because urban fields will be large, with populations of upwards of one million, their social and cultural life will form a rich and varied pattern capable of satisfying most human aspirations within a local setting.

It is no longer possible to regard the city as purely an artifact, or a political entity, or a configuration of population densities. All of these are outmoded constructs that recall a time when one could trace a sharp dividing line between town and country; between rural and urban man. From a sociological and, indeed, an economic standpoint, what is properly urban and properly rural can no longer be distinguished. The United States is becoming a thoroughly urbanized society, perhaps the first such society in history. The corresponding view of the city is no longer of a physical entity, but of a pattern of point locations and connecting flows of people, information, money, and commodities. This new understanding of the city has been incorporated into the census concept of a Standard Metropolitan Statistical Area and has since been widely accepted as a basis for public and private decisions.

The idea of an urban field is similarly based on the criterion of interdependency. It represents a fusion of metropolitan spaces and nonmetropolitan peripheral spaces centered upon core areas (SMSAs) of at least 300,000 people and extending outwards from these core areas for a distance equivalent to two hours' driving over modern throughway systems (approximately 100 miles with present technology). This represents not only an approximate geographic limit for commuting to a job, but also the limit of intensive weekend and seasonal use (by ground transportation) of the present periphery for recreation. A system of urban fields delineated by this criterion . . . [includes] between 85 and 90 per cent of the total United States population . . . while less than 35 per cent of the total land area of the country is included. These are facts of signal importance, for as the area of metropolitan influence is substantially enlarged, nearly all of us will soon be living within one or another of the 70-odd urban fields of the United States.[16]

The choice of core areas of at least 300,000 inhabitants as a basis for delineating urban fields requires some justification. Karl Fox, for instance, recommends a reduction of central city size to 25,000 or less for his proposed set of Functional Economic Areas which, in a sense, is an alternative to our concept of a system of urban fields.[17]

The threshold size of 300,000 was suggested to us by the work of Otis Dudley Duncan and his associates. According to Duncan, a Standard Metropolitan Area of 300,000 people in the United States in 1950 "marked a transition point where distinctively 'metropolitan' characteristics first begin to appear. Adequately to describe the base of the 'urban hierarchy'—consisting of almost all urban centers smaller than this size—one would have to shift the emphasis from 'metropolitanism' to other principles of functional differentiation."[18] Although the SMAs of 1950 are not equivalent to the SMSAs of 1960, the two concepts are similar enough to suggest the possibility of a transfer of Duncan's threshold size to the SMSA. An additional consideration was the expectation that core regions of this size and larger will continue to expand over the next several decades and will consequently generate a vast demand for various uses of intermetropolitan space.

The urban field of the future, however, will be a far less focussed region than today's metropolitan area. The present dominance of the metropolitan core will become attenuated as economic activities are decentralized to smaller cities within the field or into the open country, but because proximity will continue to account for a good deal of local interaction, the urban field will be a coherent region.

To define this region on a map, the main criterion should be that exchange relations *within* each field are more intensive than among them, during the course of an entire year. The calculation of this measure on an annual basis instead of at a single point in time is important because some of the functional relationships among subareas may be subject to seasonal variations. The enjoyment of summer and winter recreation areas is the outstanding example of this phenomenon. These areas should be allocated to that realm whose population makes the most intensive use of them.

It is important to recollect what this projected geographic expansion of urban living space will accomplish. First, it will turn the resources of the intermetropolitan periphery to important uses by existing metropolitan populations; second, as the periphery becomes absorbed into the urban field, it will be eliminated as a distinctive problem area. The remaining parts of the United States will either remain in low density agrarian uses or revert to wilderness for the enjoyment of distant populations.

Forces Underlying the Emergence of Urban Realms

Our case for the urban field rests on two propositions. The first is that the future growth of population in the United States will take place almost exclusively within the areas we have defined as urban fields. The second is that within each urban field substantial centrifugal forces will propel the settlement of population and the location of activities from existing metropolitan centers into the present periphery.

Continued Population Concentration in Urban Fields

One of the clearest national trends of the past few decades has been that of increasing demographic concentration. Most of the discussion, however, has emphasized the pulling together of people in metropolitan and coastal regions. It has been less well publicized that the great majority of counties that lost population during the 1950s are predominantly rural and lie outside the boundaries of any urban realm. The gains have occurred almost entirely within these boundaries, though not exclusively in metropolitan counties. We have no reason to expect this trend to be reversed during the coming generation.

In 1960, an estimated 150 million Americans lived in potential urban fields. We have projected their number to more than double the present number by the year 2000. This increase of 150 to 180 million will have to be accommodated within roughly the same area that we have provisionally delimited. The question arises as to where, within a given field, this population will be living. In approaching this question, we are mindful of the New York Metropolitan Region Study which for 1985 foresees as many people living in the "outer ring" as in the central core. This "outer ring" extends as far as 100 miles from New York City and is not today part of the daily life of the metropolis.[19] Elaborating on this startling projection, Raymond Vernon writes that employment and population trends

> cast doubt on any image of the Region as a giant cluster of human activity held together by a great nub of jobs at the center. Instead . . . [they afford] a picture of a Region in which the centripetal pull is weakening. This, in turn, means a further modification

> of the oversimplified picture of the Region as a ring of bedroom communities in the suburbs emptying out their inhabitants every morning to the central city. Incomplete and misleading as this picture is today, it promises to be even more misleading in the decades ahead. . . . And the chronic complaint of the outlying areas that they lack an "economic base" may continue to lose some of its realism and force.[20]

Vernon has foreshadowed the appearance of an urban field that would have New York City as its core. What are the forces, then, which suggest this occupancy of the periphery by people and activities, not only for New York, but for all other core regions in the United States? And what specific forms will it assume?

Centrifugal Forces: Resources of the Periphery

The main pull, we submit, is the increasing attractiveness of the periphery to metropolitan populations. It has space, it has scenery, and it contains communities that remain from earlier periods of settlement and preserve a measure of historical integrity and interest.

Demand for these resources will be generated by three main trends: increasing real income, increasing leisure, and increasing mobility. Although these trends are familiar, brief discussion of them will help to suggest their cumulative impact.

The President's Council of Economic Advisors estimates that output per man-hour may undergo a three-fold expansion by the year 2000.[21] Holding constant both working hours and labor force participation rates, this would raise average family income (in today's prices) to approximately $18,000. Although there is every reason to expect that part of the potential gains in income will be taken in the form of greater leisure through a combination of shorter working hours, longer vacations, later entry into the labor force, and earlier retirement, the prospective rise in wealth is still very substantial. If present patterns of consumption are any guide, we can expect a good share of this new wealth to be devoted to the purchase of space, privacy, travel, education, culture, and various forms of creative leisure.

The present allocation of leisure time is distributed among numerous activities. The Stanford Research Institute reports that already 50 million Americans are actively participating in amateur art activity; that 32 million are musicians, and 15 million are painters, sculptors, and sketchers. There are more piano players than fishermen, as many painters as hunters, and more theater goers than boaters, skiers, golfers, and skin-divers combined.[22]

The United States Department of Health, Education and Welfare has published statistics showing that new museums, including aquariums and zoos, are being established at the rate of one every three days, and that one-third of all existing museums in the country have been opened since 1950.[23] Other cultural activities have shown equally phenomenal gains. For instance, there are now 1400 symphony orchestras in the United States, compared to only 100 in 1920.

These new cultural facilities are more mobile, more intimate, and more dispersed than their predecessors. They are different from the grand centers of high culture left in our central cores by the nineteenth century cultural ideology.

Participation in outdoor sports is likewise on an impressive scale. In 1964, there were an estimated 38 million boaters, 20 million campers, 7 million skiers, and an equal number of golfers. Skiing enthusiasts alone have jumped by 600 percent during the past ten years. And attendance in official park and forest areas has been rising at a cumulative annual rate of about ten percent.

With increasing leisure time available, the prospects for the future show no abatement in these activities. For the mass of the people, nearly two-thirds of their waking hours will be essentially in free, unobstructured time.[24] It is therefore not surprising that the Outdoor Recreation Resources Review Commission has predicted a tripling in the overall demand for recreation by the year 2000.[25] For the hedonistic leisure society we are becoming, this estimate may indeed be a conservative one.

The combined trends in income and leisure are bound to arouse great popular interest in the periphery, but their full effect will be transmitted through the increased mobility which our technology affords.

The gradual lifting of constraints which during the industrial era packed jobs and people into tightly confined urban spaces will encourage what Jean Gottman has called the "quasi-colloidal dispersion" of activities through the urban field. Impending communications technologies suggest the possibility of relaxing the need for physical proximity in distribution, marketing, information services, and decision-making.

A few examples may be cited. Computers which keep business inventories and send information on replenishment items over TV or telephone are now technically feasible. They may also be used to alert suppliers to periodically recurring needs for product service. In retailing, a major revolution is in the making, as videophones have been developed that can transmit images of products and convert these images on signal into photographic reproductions. The use of coded cards to send information, order items, and transfer funds by telephone has already passed the laboratory stage and no doubt will soon be introduced on the market.

Transport technology continues to advance toward greater speed and versatility. Supersonic and short-distance jets, automated highways, and rail transport which moves at several hundred miles an hour through densely built-up regions, are expected to pass from drawing board to commercial application within ten to twenty years. The result will be a further shrinkage of the transportation surface and vastly increased accessibility on a national scale no less than within each urban field.

One effect of increased accessibility especially worthy of note is the estimated 3.5 to 7.5 million acres which will be opened up for urban development when the federal interstate highway program is completed. This land newly available for urbanization will represent a major resource to the national economy.

The combined effects of greater income, leisure, and mobility will be felt, by virtue of these arguments, primarily on the present periphery of metropolitan regions, as demand for the use of its resources are vastly intensified. Some of these uses are shown in Table 3.1. They are distinctly urban in character. And they remind us of Lewis Mumford's prophetic vision of the "Invisible City."

> Gone is primitive local monopoly through isolation: gone is the metropolitan monopoly through seizure and exploitation. . . . The ideal mission of the city is to further [a] process of cultural circulation and diffusion; and this will restore to many now subordinate urban centers a variety of activities that were once drained away for the exclusive benefit of the great city.[26]

Emerging Life Styles of the Urban Fields

The projected incorporation of the periphery into the urban realm will be accompanied by significant changes in American

Table 3.1: *Uses of the Intermetropolitan Periphery*

RECREATION	COMMUNITIES
camps	holiday communities
parks	retirement communities
forests	vacation villages
wilderness areas	art colonies
nature sanctuaries	diversified "new towns"
resorts	historical communities
outdoor sport areas	second home areas
quietist retreats	
INSTITUTIONS	ECONOMIC ACTIVITIES
boarding schools	agro-business
junior colleges	space-extensive manufacturing plants
universities	research and communication-based industries
museums	mail order houses
cultural centers	warehouses
scientific research stations	insurance companies
conference centers	jet airports
hospitals	
sanatoria	
government administrative offices	

patterns of living. On the whole, we expect that these changes will be evaluated favorably. Derogatory slogans, such as "sprawl" and "scatteration," bandied about in ideological campaigns, will have to be discarded in any serious search for what it means to live on the new scale. Although not all the consequences can be foreseen now, a few merit closer attention. We shall restrict our comment to only three of them: a wider life space on the average, a wider choice of living environments, and a wider community of interests.

1. *A wider life space.* The effective life space of an individual includes all the geographic areas within which his life unfolds. It includes his home and its immediate vicinity; his place of work or schooling; the places in which he does his shopping and engages in leisure activities; the more distant places to which he travels for business, recreation, or learning; the residence areas of the friends and relatives he visits; and the connecting paths over which he travels to reach his destination.

It is possible to map these spaces for individuals—distinguished by age, sex, and socio-economic status—as well as for entire communities. These maps would show which areas of the total available space are actually being used by different parts of the population as well as the intensity of their use. An important feature of these maps would be data relating to the percentage of the individual's total annual time spent at different localities and travelling over various routes. A further distinction with regard to the seasonability of use could be made.

Such maps for an urban field would reveal greatly expanded and more complexly structured systems of life spaces for the total population compared to existing patterns. The higher speeds, greater versatility, and lower costs expected in transportation and communication during the next few decades will encourage a dispersion of people and activities throughout the urban field and a further thinning out of metropolitan core areas on an unsurpassed scale. Technological innovations will make it possible to substitute mobility for location. The strong likelihood that this will occur is suggested by foreseeable changes in patterns which underlie the location decisions of families and firms.

For individual families, locational decisions will be increasingly influenced by larger incomes that will permit the purchase of more space, more privacy, and more transportation; by a growing concern with the qualitative aspects of life, especially with the quality of the physical environment; by the gradual relaxation of the puritanical distinction between work and play, especially among professional and business elite groups; and by the desire for an environment that will permit a richer family life. All of these forces will tend to render the intermetropolitan periphery more attractive as a place to live, and help to tie it more closely into the urban field.

The location of business firms will encounter fewer economic constraints within the urban field than at present. This is especially true for the new kinds of service activities—professional, managerial, research- and communications-based—which are the leading edge of a post-industrial society. Urban infrastructure and services will be nearly ubiquitous throughout the urban field; the pressing need for physical propinquity among firms is declining; and the expansion and improvement of transport and communication services will tend to make regional as well as national markets equally accessible. If only those economic factors that operate generally throughout a given field are taken into account, thereby excluding local subsidies or differences in local tax structure, which provide only small and temporary advantages, it is possible to assert that firms may locate nearly at random throughout the field, subject only to the constraint of labor force distribution. Location of the labor force will then become a primary determinant in business location decisions, with the result that firms will be attracted in increasing numbers into what is now the intermetropolitan periphery. Firms as well as families will substitute mobility and machine-interposed communications for location.

2. *A wider choice of living environments both for resident and non-resident use and more frequent interchange among environments.* The urban field offers a heterogeneous landscape, consisting of metropolitan cores, small towns, and varied open spaces.[27] Within it, a wide variety of living environments may

be sought and created. There is nothing rigid or predetermined about the physical form of the field: rather, it may be viewed as a mosaic of different forms and micro-environments which coexist within a common communications framework without intruding spatially on each other.

For the family, the urban field offers a far greater choice of living environments than do the old metropolitan areas. Alternatives include country and in-town living, perhaps combined, through a steep increase in the frequency of second homes for year-round use; single family dwellings and apartment towers; dense metropolitan clusters and open countryside; new towns and towns with an historical tradition; and functionally specialized communities.

No part within the urban field is isolated from another. There is rather an easy-going interchange among all the parts, encouraged not only by the wider distribution of population but also by the larger amounts of time available for the pursuit of leisure. All areas are located no further than two hours' driving distance from old metropolitan cores. And although these cores will lose much of their present importance to the people of the field as functions are decentralized, they will continue for at least a few more decades to attract many people to the activities that are traditionally carried out within them, such as major educational and governmental institutions, famous museums, outstanding music, artistic, and sport events. Many cultural facilities, however, will be dispersed throughout the realm and many metropolitan services will become available at any point within it through extended distribution systems. At the same time, easy access to other urban fields can be provided through a regional system of airports capable of handling short-distance jets and vertical take-off craft. High-speeds rail transport may be a significant means for inter-realm travel in some parts of the country, such as the "Northeast Corridor."

3. *A wider community of interests.* The already noted increase in the effective life space of the population suggests that each person will have interests in happenings over a larger segment of the field than at present. In the course of a year, he may

actively participate in the life of a number of spatially defined local communities. As a result, he is likely to be less concerned with the fate of the community where he resides and more with activities that may be scattered throughout the field but are closest to his interests, leading to a stronger identification on his part with the realm as a whole at the cost of a declining interest in purely local affairs. (In some places, this loss may be offset by the smaller size of his resident community which would encourage more active participation in problem-solving.) We foresee continuation of the present trend toward a cosmopolitanization of values, attitudes, and behavior, with politically relevant behavior organized principally along functional lines, and with the governing of local communities (places) passing increasingly into the hands of professionals.

Implications for Public Policy

In the preceding sections of this essay, we have speculated openly about the future. The urban field would emerge as a normal consequence of the forces that are currently operating on the space economy of the United States. Its designation as an ecological unit, however, is purely conceptual: it is only one of the many spatial patterns that might have been recognized. Specifically, its choice was dictated by our belief in the utility of the urban field as an appropriate region for planning. The vastly enlarged scale of urban living we envisage for the future holds clear implications for public action. We shall comment on only two of these: actions to reinforce existing trends toward the incorporation of the inter-metropolitan periphery into the urban field and actions that will assure the environmental integrity of all activities within the field.

1. *Reinforcement of existing trends.* We have portrayed the emergence of the urban field in approving language. We might have spoken out, as others have, against the rootlessness of modern man, the loss of community, and the misfortune of urban sprawl. Our words, however, were carefully selected; they repre-

sent our conviction that there is, indeed, a social good to be obtained from the substitution of mobility for location. Not only is the urban field the living environment most consistent with the aims of a wealthy leisure society, it will also help to reverse the steady deterioration of the periphery; and this we see as a major social objective. There are losses as well as gains to be incurred by allowing the expansion of metropolis into the periphery, but we believe the gains will outweigh the losses. Political considerations strengthen this judgment: it would be difficult in the extreme to change the direction of existing trends and squeeze an urban population to be doubled in size within the next thirty years into the confines of existing metropolitan areas. We conclude that public policy should in this instance "cooperate with the inevitable" and support the penetration of the inter-metropolitan periphery by forms of urban life.

Governments can exercise two modes of influence to hasten the arrival of urban fields: the first is the location of government-financed investments; the second is information. The former is perhaps the more persuasive in the long view. There is a singular opportunity for planning on the scale of urban fields in the design of regional highway and railroad systems, in the location and design of regional airports, in the siting of regional colleges and government-sponsored research institutions, in the distribution of administrative offices, and in the designation and development of public land reserves for recreation. Somewhat less direct controls over location can be used in connection with subsidy programs for the acquisition of second homes as well as for the building of retirement communities and new towns.

To contribute to the emergence of urban fields, determination of public and private locations should occur within an adequate framework of information. The potential reality of the urban field should be captured in statistical series and maps. As a first step, the boundaries of the realm must be empirically ascertained on the basis of careful studies of daily, weekly, and seasonal flow patterns and tested against a gravity model. It is clear that the boundaries so delimited for statistical purposes will be shifting over time as the region begins to be more fully developed, transportation technology advances, and the inevitable phenomenon of zones transitional to adjacent fields is better understood. Once the region has been roughly defined, its present uses and potential assets should be investigated and evaluated against the changing pattern of metropolitan demands, with particular attention to the trends of change in spatial structure. These investigations would culminate in a general regional development plan as a guide to location decisions. The plan which, like all good plans, would need to be constantly in elaboration, would suggest broad land use patterns as well as desirable new investments, public and private. The final step would involve the establishment of an information and monitoring system for the realm to maintain close watch over regional changes as they occur.

2. *Assuring environmental integrity.* If the urban field is to be developed as a meaningful living environment, it is essential that its manifold uses do not encroach upon each other and in the process destroy its most valuable assets: open space, scenic attractiveness, and historical tradition. Indiscriminate metropolitan growth should be minimized; new towns should be selected with attention to the total pattern of land uses and the evolving distribution of population, activities, and transportation. Cultural institutions should be so located as to reinforce other forms of recreation, present and contemplated. Areas for agricultural production should be set aside, not only for economic reasons, but also to provide a richer visual and environmental experience to the inhabitants of the realm.

Assuring an appropriate environmental setting for each activity (or bundle of activities) in the field will involve something more than the judicious application of traditional land use controls, though no doubt these will be necessary. It will require forthright programs of area development and resource conservation, including the preservation of old townscapes and the more outstanding features of the rural landscape.

A suggestion for this type of program is provided by experience in France. "Throughout France, the fast-spreading ownership of automobiles is making it possible to restore and maintain the rural villages that are so much a part of her charm. A national inventory of abandoned houses is published, and liberal government credits are given to purchasers who restore them. In recent years, thousands of old country homes have become summer houses for city people. Whole villages have come to life again."[28] Much can be done at the national or state level to encourage the repossession of the intermetropolitan periphery in view of the varied uses proposed for it within the urban field.

The institutional basis for developmental planning in the urban field will have to face up to new constraints that will limit social decision-making. These include the multiplication of governments, (not 1400 as in New York but perhaps 4000!), overlapping jurisdictions and responsibilities, the increasing functional rather than spatial orientation of interests among the population, the gradual loosening of communal ties, the fuzziness of field boundaries, lagging citizen response to the enlarged scale of living, and the extension of urban fields into adjacent states as well as the continuing conflicts of values, (public versus private, conservationist versus expansionary, traditionalist versus modern, residential versus productive). No easy rationalization of the planning process is possible under these conditions nor, perhaps, is it desirable. If metropolitan-wide planning is only now coming into being—decades after the "discovery" of the metropolitan region as the new urban scale, and just when this scale is about to be replaced by the even broader concept of the urban realm—it seems futile to argue for the exclusiveness of the urban field as a planning unit. Field planning will have to coexist with other forms. Primary responsibility for the development of urban fields will unquestionably come to rest with the states; but this is only a beginning. The federal government will have a role to play as important as that of local governments, while interstate and intercommunity cooperation in developmental planning will become much more common than it is at present. The coordination of these different levels of planning presents a major problem that must be solved through both formal and informal methods of program cooperation. The formulation of a regional development plan in joint consultation with all the relevant parties will be necessary to provide the common framework for decisions.

A Challenge of Mounting Urgency

It would indeed be a pity if our era were to fail in taking advantage of the great opportunities which the dynamism and tensions of our society are creating for building a new urban culture. The expansionary forces that suggest the possibility of urban fields are irreversible; what we make of them is our choice. They could well terminate in the desecration of the urban landscape, in a grey formlessness, the spoliation of resources. In place of designing an environment for exuberant living, we could acquiesce in the gradual attrition of life by neglecting to take the appropriate measures now. The pattern of the urban field will elude easy perception by the eye and will be difficult to rationalize in terms of a Euclidean geometry. It will be a large complex pattern which, unlike the traditional city, will no longer be directly accessible to the senses. We might think of it rather as a time-space continuum that must first be reduced to a meaningful abstract model before it will submit to being managed as a whole. Such models are not yet in sight. But the challenge to search for them confronts the planning profession with mounting urgency.

NOTES

1. Max Weber, *The City* (Glencoe, Illinois: The Free Press, 1958), p. 62.
2. Clarence S. Stein, "A Regional Pattern for Dispersal," *Architectural Record,* CXXXVI (September, 1964), 205–206.
3. Frank Lloyd Wright, *The Living City* (New York: Horizon Press, Inc., 1958).
4. The review is being conducted by the Social Science Research Council Committee on Areas for Social and Economic Statistics.
5. *Christian Science Monitor,* 14 November, 1964, p. 3.
6. Jean Gottmann, *Megalopolis* (New York: The Twentieth Century Fund, Inc. 1961).
7. Herman C. Berkman, *Our Urban Plant: Essays in Urban Affairs* (Madison, Wisconsin: The University of Wisconsin Extension, 1964), pp. 4–5.

8. The final stage in the hierarchy of living spaces. See for example, "The Ekistic Grid" *Ekistics,* XIX (March, 1965), 210.
9. Catherine Bauer Wurster, "The Form and Structure of the Future Urban Complex," in Lowdon Wingo, Jr. (ed.), *Cities and Space* (Baltimore: The Johns Hopkins Press for Resources for the Future, Inc. 1963), p. 73.
10. ARA eligibility criteria are rather complicated. They are fully stated in U.S. Department of Commerce, Area Redevelopment Administration, *Summary List of Redevelopment Areas and Eligible Areas, Public Works Acceleration Act* (Washington, D.C.: U.S. Government Printing Office, 1964), p. 2.
11. Ray M. Northam, "Declining Urban Centers in the United States: 1950–1960," *Annals of the Association of American Geographers,* LIII (March, 1963), 50–59.
12. Appalachian Regional Commission, *Appalachia* (Washington, D.C.: U. S. Government Printing Office, 1964).
13. U. S. Department of Agriculture, *Recent Population Trends in the United States with Emphasis on Rural Areas,* Agricultural Economic Report No. 23 (1963), pp. 24–25.
14. Harry M. Caudill has documented this physical and social deterioration of declining intermetropolitan peripheral areas in his able study of eastern Kentucky, *Night Comes to the Cumberlands* (Boston: Little, Brown & Company, 1962). See especially Chapter Twenty: "The Scene Today," pp. 325–351. Evidence that this is not an isolated phenomenon exists for other intermetropolitan peripheral areas. The *New York Times,* 21 March, 1965, reports that "hundreds of Texas towns and smaller cities that once drew incomes from agriculture are finding few farmers left today to trade in their stores and banks. Massive depopulation has been the rule." Only where agressive local leadership in a few communities has grasped opportunities in regional and national markets has the decline been decelerated. According to the University of Texas Bureau of Business Research, regional and national corporations are not attracted to invest in these communities. Disintegration of morale, physical facilities, and the economic climate was also characteristic of large parts of the intermetropolitan periphery of Western Massachusetts within the dynamic "megalopolis" described by Gottmann. A regional study of this area by M.I.T. students elicited a general expression of disintegrating community through the comments of local citizens. "People feel," as one citizen volunteered, "it is a second rate town. Young people get it from their parents." "The people move out, leave their houses vacant, and after awhile they look dingy." "We are in a rut. We have an inferiority complex." "Young people don't plan to stay." "Look at those vacancies on main street. It's depressing." "The people who should be leading just are not." "Leadership. Business people think it is a thankless job—don't want any part of it."
15. The Economic Research Service of the U.S. Department of Agriculture in a study of the effects of metropolitan growth trends on rural counties asserts that "the existence of a large, dense, and growing urban population in a region tends to create conditions of population growth in rural counties of the same region. This is true not only because an ever larger number of the rural counties are within commuting range of urban centers, but also because more distant counties are affected by the accession of businesses or residents who

do not need frequent commutation to the city but whose work or choice of residence is related to the city—especially the large metropolitan city. These are counties beyond 'exurbia' which the geographer Wilbur Zelinsky has referred to as the 'urban penumbra.'" *Op. cit.*, p. 14.

16. It is significant to note that if all present SMSA's of between 200,000 and 300,000 people were to reach the critical threshold size of 300,000 during the next generation, only a small expansion of the area now included in urban realms would occur. Most of these centers are located within or close to the edge of an existing urban realm and are thus encompassed by the boundaries we have provisionally defined.
17. For his most recent statement, see Karl Fox, "Programs for Economic Growth in Non-Metropolitan Areas," paper prepared for the Third Conference on Regional Accounts, Miami Beach, Florida, November 19–21, 1964.
18. Otis D. Duncan et al., *Metropolis and Region* (Baltimore: The Johns Hopkins Press for Resources for the Future, Inc., 1960), p. 275.
19. The Core (New York City's four major boroughs and Hudson County) total population in 1985 is estimated by Vernon to be 7,810,000, a decline of almost half a million from the 1955 population. The Outer Ring (90 minutes from Manhattan to up to 30 miles beyond that) total is given to be 7,809,000, an increase of over 300 percent. Raymond Vernon, *Metropolis 1985* (Cambridge, Massachusetts: Harvard University Press, 1960), p. 221.
20. *Ibid.*, p. 224.
21. President's Council of Economic Advisers, *1964 Annual Report,* as reported in the *Christian Science Monitor,* 28 January, 1965.
22. As reported by Ralph Lazarus, "An 'Age of Fulfillment,'" in the *Christian Science Monitor,* 6 February 1964.
23. As reported by Josephine Ripley, "U.S. Cultural Crescendo," in the *Christian Science Monitor,* 1 January 1965.
24. The National Planning Association has projected an average work week of only 30 hours for the year 2000.
25. Outdoor Recreation Resources Review Commission, *Action for Outdoor Recreation for America* (Washington: Citizen's Committee for the ORRC Report, 1964), p. 8.
26. Lewis Mumford, *The City in History* (New York: Harcourt, Brace and World, Inc., 1961), p. 564.
27. It will be recalled that the definition of an urban field is based on a metropolitan center of at least 300,000 inhabitants. From this it follows that an urban field may include within its perimeter smaller metropolitan areas as well as "satellite" cities of varying size up to the size of the metropolitan core area.
28. Archie Robertson, "Europe Moves to the Suburbs," *The Lamp,* XLVII (Spring, 1965), 29.

4 *The Rising Demand for Urban Amenities*

JEAN GOTTMAN

A French geographer whose study of the urbanized northeastern seaboard gave currency to the concept of megalopolis, *Jean Gottman finds that the most rapidly growing urban areas are the megalopolitan clusters and urban areas in parts of the country that resemble the Riviera in the opportunities they provide for leisure activities. Because, he argues, these trends reflect underlying tendencies that cannot readily be controlled, the future shape of urban America will depend upon how public policy copes with the continuing movement of population into megalopolis and the Rivieras of the south, southwest, and west.*

[In 1964] the President of the United States sent a message to Congress on the problems and future of American cities, which, in its preamble, quoted the famous statement by Aristotle in his *Politics:* "Men come together in cities in order to live. They remain together in order to live the good life."[1]

Urban life has always conveyed at one and the same time an idea of superior quality in the mode of living ("urbane," "urbanity") and also a hint at the difficulties and social problems in the process of organization and growth. This duality of contrasted characteristics of urban life has led philosophers, preachers, and politicians to express preferences for the small town or at least a not too large city. Such a middle-of-the-road solution appears

Reprinted from Sam Bass Warner (ed.), *Planning for a Nation of Cities,* pp. 163–77, by permission of the M.I.T. Press, Cambridge, Massachusetts.

less and less practicable today. There were, by 1800, only seven cities in the world grouping half a million people or more. There are more than two hundred of them today. Two million people agglomerated in one urban district appeared an extraordinary phenomenon a century ago; there are about seventy such urban concentrations today; and this number of very large cities is bound to grow fast. The President's recent message also forecast: "A half century from now 320 million of our 400 million Americans will live in such areas. And our *largest cities* will receive the greatest impact of growth" [our italics].

There is urgent need to examine the problem of planning for better urban life. There is rather wide consensus that present conditions are not good, that they are worsening, and that little has as yet been seriously attempted to arrest the decay and start improving the urban environment. Also, the solution adopted widely by the many who could afford it, that is, the flight to the suburbs, appears about to be reaching its limits in the larger metropolitan areas. The difficulties of transportation, especially for commuters, the worsening general conditions of scattered suburban life have spurred the search for new, different ways of improving urban life. Increasingly the opinion has been expressed that modern Western society in general, and the American nation especially, should be able to manage better the conditions and modes of their urban life; contemporary affluence, technology, and social consciousness ought to combine to solve the existing problems. It is also felt that improving housing, purity of the air and of the water, policing of the city, transportation, schools, and other services will not be enough, and cannot suffice, if treated piecemeal. A general plan for a "good life" is wished for.

The Conference at Washington University examined many of the specific trends affecting urban life; the debates demonstrated much dedicated soul-searching on the possibilities of achieving fuller employment, higher incomes, better integration, and so forth. Most of the search developed in the two areas at present in the limelight of the national political scene, that is, race relations and civil rights on the one hand, and the war on poverty on the other. These considerations are certainly basic to the quality of urban life in America, and in many other countries today. In a way, it could be observed that the conference debated *"urbi et orbi,"* extending the perspectives of urban life to the "Great Society" as a whole. In a nation where 93 percent of the people draw their incomes from nonagricultural pursuits, such attitudes are understandable. One wonders nevertheless at the more special needs and means of the large cities and metropolitan areas; these, because of their size, of the density of population and of activities achieved there, have specific characteristics and problems. General affluence and civil good behavior do not solve specifically urban problems, although it ought to be easier to arrive at satisfactory solutions amid such economic and social advantages.

A better quality of urban life suggests abundant and widespread physical and cultural amenities made available to the city dwellers. The contemporary process of urbanization has not often provided for such amenities in the various cities and metropolitan areas. Although it has been accompanied by a rise in the standards of living and generalized affluence for a majority (the war on poverty has really focused on only one fifth of the American nation), urbanization has caused in recent years more pollution, not only of the air and water, but also of the landscape. Slums and junkyards are only two factors of "landscape pollution" among many; the decaying old business districts of many cities, old and blighted industrial or warehousing buildings, ugly and poorly maintained wharves, tracks, railway stations, etc., are all important factors in the picture. What is called for is not simply preservation of the old cityscapes with which old memories have embroiled our emotions. In the fast-changing environment of these days, "the shape of a city changes faster, alas, than a mortal's heart," as Charles Baudelaire said, in the midst of the sweeping renewal of Paris by Haussmann in the 1850's. Our means for molding spaces and materials are greater now than ever; they call for a rapidly changing urban morphology, bringing more amenities, and an actually good life, into the cities.

The profession of planners in America has the reputation of

attaching little importance to the physical amenities in urban design. Of Alberti's famous duality of the qualities required in the townscape, *"commoditas et voluptas,"* only the former, meaning functionalism, efficiency, has apparently retained the attention of Americans. Many critics of the modern city in America have eloquently bemoaned this attitude of the planners. The constructive proposals offered by such critics have remained too often in the realm of conservation of monuments of yesterday and of the preservation of a status quo where it seemed still socially and esthetically satisfactory. This was the slowly evolving mood of the common mortal's heart, lacking realization of the dynamic momentum of this era. If in many respects man is a creature of habit, he is also and will remain a creature of progress and capricious fashion. Changes in urban and architectural design must follow the evolution of society's structure, of the common man's occupations and use of time, his aspirations and endeavors. In fact, where careful design has been applied, town planning in America has produced remarkable good results, thus the college campus, a major American contribution to modern urban design.

The style of the half century to come may be deduced to some extent from some of the obvious trends of present American society. We do not pretend to forecast the precise plastic characteristics of future fashions in the arts of living and building, but we may outline where the demand for styles of living and location is headed for. In fact, it has been on the way there for some little while.

Americans have always been mobile, and in recent years, owing to improved means of transportation, they have been very much on the move. Where have they been moving to? The statistics of migration within the United States are very telling. On one hand, most of the growing population has been gathering increasingly into the metropolitan areas. Although the total acreage of the latter has been expanding, a higher proportion of the population is now concentrating on a rather small percentage of the total land area. More square miles have their population thinned out than there are square miles on which the population is thickening. Despite the visual impressions created by the suburban sprawl, Americans are on the move to live in higher density formations than in the past. The regions being thinned out are not deserted; their lands and buildings remain quite productive; but small fractions of the land area are harboring increasingly a higher percentage of the total population.

Megalopolis, the huge urbanized area on the northeastern seaboard, in 1950 contained 21.2 percent of the nation on 1.8 percent of the land area of the conterminous United States;[2] in 1960 in this same area the population represented a slightly lower proportion of the nation, 20.5 percent, but its number had risen from 32 million in 1950 to 37 million in 1960, or by 5 million, meaning a serious increase in average density (from 596 to 688 inhabitants per square mile). If the nation as a whole had grown slightly faster (by 18.5 percent) in that decade and if the attraction of Megalopolis seemed to be weakening, other regions had considerably increased their share of the total population: California saw its population rise by 48.5 percent and Florida by 78.7 percent. These two states aggregated 8.8 percent of the United States total population in 1950 and 11.4 percent in 1960. Most of these increases had thickened the population on less than half of the land area of these two states. Heavy densities were forming there, as in Megalopolis. At the three corners of the national territory small fractions of it held 32 per cent of the nation[3] in 1960 on less than 5 percent of the area, as compared with 30 percent in 1950. This trend will probably be accelerated through the 1960's.

It is interesting to look at the figures of the net migration of whites (who have had freer choice of where to live) by States within the United States since 1940. A few regions, all distributed on the periphery of the country have attracted most of the net interstate migration of whites from 1940 to 1962:[4] the Southwest (mainly California and Arizona) and Megalopolis (i.e., the northeastern seaboard states, mainly from Connecticut to Virginia); two smaller but notable other corners of the country show a great and continuous power of attraction: Florida (fastest growing of all states) and the State of Washington. Finally, Texas and Ohio also attract migrants, though in thinner and less regular fashion.

With the exception of Ohio, the net migration obviously flows toward areas at the periphery of the national territory that are richly endowed with either cultural or physical amenities, or both, as is now the case of California, which has received the most massive inflow for the last thirty years. That the "geography of amenities"[5] plays an important part in the selection of location for people and a number of industries is increasingly recognized by students of statistics and by business managers. The lure of climate and landscape used to attract the wealthy, the people of leisure, the aged who could afford it. Thus the fortune began of the "Rivieras" in France and Italy, of the Californian and Floridian costs in America. Now these areas are bustling with young, busy people, and with a variety of economic activities.

Such migrations of people and of job opportunities are not observed in the United States only. Similar trends are clearly at work in Britain (where a recent article is entitled "Shall we all go to live in the Southeast?"), in France (where the major growth areas are those of Greater Paris and the Mediterranean seashore from Monte Carlo to Marseille), in the Netherlands (where decentralization policies could not prevent the attraction to the Randstadt Holland encircling Amsterdam, The Hague and Rotterdam), in Switzerland (towards the Zurich-Basle and Geneva-Lausanne areas), and in most of the other fairly developed countries of Europe, Asia, and the Americas. The rapidly growing urban regions of the world may be, in most cases, grouped into the major categories which could be designated the "megalopolitan category" and the "Riviera category."

By "megalopolitan" is meant a category of urban regions formed around one or several large cities which arose as centers of commerce, industry, and perhaps government, and still are such centers. By "Rivieras" is meant another category, whose growth has been chiefly due to the advantages the area offered for recreational activities. One does not need to insist at great length today on the recreational advantages provided by the physical amenities found on the French and Italian Rivieras, in Southern California or on the "Gold Coast" of Florida; they have been advertised enough throughout the world in order to attract first, tourists, then residents, and finally industries. "Rivieras" grew by putting to work a set of attractive factors quite different from those of the "megalopolitan" areas. It is noteworthy, however, that in the past centuries, commercial, industrial, and governmental functions have always favored the formation and expansion of urban centers, but that recreation is a new function for large, growing urban areas; the Riviera type of urban ribbon is special to recent times and mainly to the twentieth century. As they expand, they also bring commercial and industrial business into the beautiful region, which had only physical amenities to start with. Cultural amenities follow. The Rivieras may extend also to encompass old centers of trade. Thus new large urban areas arise, which may ultimately acquire characteristics similar to those of urban regions of "megalopolitan" origin. "Rivieras," however, are likely to care more about the looks of their environment, as they know better from experience the economic value of attractive surroundings.

The massive economic success of regions richly endowed with physical amenities seems a logical development at a time of rising standards of living, lengthening of leisure time for the mass, greater mobility of people, and better education for all. These four trends concur in fostering the congregation of people in those areas where they will find a more pleasant life and broader opportunity. Megalopolitan regions usually offer the opportunity; they also have worked hard to provide at least some physical amenities. The original Megalopolis on the northeastern seaboard of the United States had the need and the means to provide recreational areas near its sprawling cities to serve the leisure of its urban crowds. Coney Island was a start that became a popular image; but Atlantic City, the Catskills, Cape Cod with its neighboring islands, and many other parks and resorts were formed within Megalopolis itself or nearby. These local facilities are helpful but do not satisfy the swelling demand for more recreational amenities and of better taste.

The increasing concentration of population in a few urban areas, large in comparison with the old concept of a city but small as a fraction of the nation's whole territory, is an understandable trend. It began in fact with the industrial revolution and the flow of the labor force from the farms to the cities. But it takes on a sharper, more selective form, which threatens to decrease considerably the relative importance of the population in most of the national system with the exception of the faster growing areas. The parts of the country being thinned out do not like this prospect. In most well-developed countries legislation has been passed opposing the trends of concentration, aiming at a more equal distribution of the population over all the land, and in any case endeavoring to maintain the present distribution.

This legislation varies from country to country. It was started, in fact, early in this century with the purpose of limiting the exodus from the farms, and helping the small family farm to survive and prosper. Legislators often believed that the family farm was the staunchest pillar of democracy, of political stability. There was widespread distrust of the crowds of workers gathering in the cities. Thus, in the United States and in Western Europe, farmers were granted various advantages in terms of taxation, price supports for their products, and subsidies. Electoral districts were designed to favor the stable rural areas in the distribution of seats in legislative assemblies. The electoral weight of farming areas in the House of Commons has often been emphasized, though farmers account for less than 5 percent of the total population of Britain. The current debate on legislative reapportionment in the United States well illustrates how the designing of districts has favored for a long time the rural areas losing in proportion to the total population.

Such measures, which have been fairly generally adopted in the democracies on both sides of the North Atlantic, were aimed at advantaging the rual areas, in order to convince their populations to stay where they were. Greater political influence gave them the economic means of improving their opportunities at home, making these regions more attractive to their residents and even to in-migrants. At the same time, by restricting the growth of political influence of the rapidly expanding urban regions, these same measures seemed appropriate to discourage at least some of the process of concentration, reputed politically and socially evil. These calculations were correct, but they failed to achieve their main goal: the major concentrations and a few new ones continued growing at an accelerated rate, both in figures of population and in employment opportunity. Megalopolis, California and Florida in the United States, metropolitan Toronto, Montreal, and Vancouver in Canada, Greater London and the Southeast around it in Britain, Greater Paris in France, the Randstadt Holland in the Netherlands, Greater Stockholm in Sweden, the Zurich-Basle-Berne triangle in Switzerland, the Milan-Turin area in Italy, etc. The countries at large complained that these metropolises were sucking up all their blood.

Then sterner legislative measures were proposed and in some cases approved. New regulations forbade new industrial establishments and even office buildings to come to the central cities or even regions of these areas whose growth seemed to be upsetting the existing political and economic balance of the country. Paris, Amsterdam, London have now lived for almost twenty years under rules, gradually tightening, aimed at strangling their growth. Some economic activities were thus induced to go elsewhere. The growth of these areas of "megalopolitan type" was probably slower as a result than if these rules had not been applied. Various activities in the cities and suburbs were inconvenienced by these rules. But it turned out to be impossible to enforce them fully. Growth went on. People continued to congregate in and around the condemned areas, creating more congestion there. Many plants or offices forced to look for another location found a site in another area of fast growth. Those that failed to obtain a permit in Greater Paris went to Amsterdam or The Hague, Geneva or Zurich, or to the Marseille-Riviera seaboard of southeast France. The central plateau and some of the southwest of France kept on losing population as previously. Similar examples could be cited in other countries.

The failure of political pressure and stern legislation to stop a trend of concentration in small areas, which elect only a minority of the various legislative bodies, forcefully demonstrates the power of the economic, social, and psychological forces at work in modern society and shaping contemporary urbanization. Basic to this process is the occupational evolution bringing about, gradually and quietly, a profound economic and social revolution, one of which most people are not yet aware.

The industrial revolution began long ago to reduce the labor force needed on the farms and gather more workers in teeming cities and towns to work in mines, manufacturing plants, warehouses, seaports, and on the railroads. As the work of mining and manufacturing became increasingly mechanized and automated, fewer people at work produced greater quantities of goods at lesser cost. In the United States the evolution of the labor force is more advanced in this respect than in any other large country, and this evolution has greatly accelerated in recent years. From 1950 to 1964, the number of production workers employed in manufacturing has remained rather stable, oscillating around the figure of 12.5 million. Meanwhile, the total number of employees in nonagricultural establishments increased by about 13 million (from 45.2 to 58.5), that is, by as large a number of jobs as there were engaged in producing the huge manufacturing output of this country. But this rapid increase of 13 million employees was not found in mining (employment in which fell), or in transportation and public utilities (total employment in which oscillated during those 15 years around 4 million) or, once more, in manufacturing production. Although the quantities of goods produced and handled greatly increased in the same period (by about 68 per cent), the number of people actually occupied in production and handling work did not increase; the productivity of their labor did. The new 13 million jobs were found in such fields as wholesale and retail trade (registering an increase of 3 million jobs), finance, insurance, and real estate (plus 1 million), miscellaneous services (plus 3 million), and government (plus 4 million, mainly on local and state governments). By 1963, these four growing sectors of the labor force totaled 32.6 million employees, more than half of the total nonagricultural employment. At the same time, the figure of the nonproduction employment of the manufacturing industries (i.e., managerial, office, research workers, etc.) rose by 1.8 million (from 2.7 million in 1950 to 4.5 million in 1963). Obviously, the future of the labor force is in the nonproduction areas, in specialized and advanced services: Megalopolis on the northeastern seaboard has shown an advanced thrust in that direction, as we demonstrated in our study of this region.[6] Similar statistical trends are shaping up in most countries of Western Europe and in Japan.

We have now embarked on a new economic period which we may call the "white collar revolution." It heralds the passage of the bulk of the labor force into clean work requiring qualified skills, responsibility, continuing education. It means shorter work days and perhaps work weeks, more vacation time; therefore a much greater demand for *education* on one hand, *recreation* on the other (rather than actual leisure, for the white-collar worker often has to think about his work while away from it). For such a society, the modes of living will be substantially different from those determined by the industrial revolution of yesterday.

First of all, manufacturing and storage plants, which used to congregate in the cities and form the bases of urban growth, no longer need this concentration. As they employ fewer hands, they do not require large residential groupings in their immediate vicinity. Industrial and warehousing plants can now scatter along the railways and highways; they no longer congregate in cities or dense formations by necessity. Only a few categories of industrial establishments still need the proximity of one another or of a large market. The cities are losing their "black country" and busy manufacuring appearance of the industrial revolution period. In the white-collar era they can afford another, cleaner, more elegant look.

The second force now at play is the interdependence, still very strong, of those qualified services (we suggested calling them "quaternary activities" in our study of Megalopolis) which are growing fast and begin to form a sizable portion of the total labor force; that is, the administration of public and private affairs, the financial community, research and higher education, mass media and advertising, highly specialized professional services, style-setting recreational and artistic activities. These are all very tightly interwoven in their daily operation; to function well, business management needs government; they both need easy access to the best available information, research, specialized consultants' advice, higher education, and entertainment. The interconnections and complementarity of these economic, social, and cultural activities have always been important, and they made large metropolises grow in every lively civilized country. Now these activities are becoming major sectors of employment and, insofar as mechanization and automation will stay and grow with us, this trend does not seem reversible in the forseeable future.

The managerial, recreational, and mass media functions are not only offering more jobs nowadays, but they have glamour and prestige; and they contribute an exciting element to the growing city of tomorrow. This special factor is important. It attracts a certain quality of manpower that could have the choice between several jobs in different locations. The story is now well known of the large corporation offices which considered moving out of Manhattan after World War II; they gave up this plan because of the difficulty of finding the quality of employees they wanted in the various scattered locations under consideration. The IBM Corporation built its largest European center at La Gaude, near Nice, in an extremely beautiful site of the French Riviera, largely to offer the young scientists and technicians they employ all the advantages of living and working amid the physical, cultural, and recreational amenities of this glamourous spot of Europe.

Many more examples of this trend, now general in the advanced countries, could be cited. There is little doubt that as the new generation enters the labor force in the coming years, better educated, aiming at employment in the growing and more fashionable sectors of the economy, there will be an increasing concentration around the urban regions that will develop the most pleasant mode of life, and offer a wide and attractive gamut of amenities. Such local conditions are largely man-made; they require a great deal of enthusiastic planning, investment, and care.

The traditional definition of the geographical region called a "Riviera" was that it is a seaboard where the mountains come close to the shore and that it is generally oriented toward the southeast. That means the amenities of sea, mountain, and a sunny climate all together. In Italy, however, the necessity of the southeastern orientation was discarded in calling two regions, one "Riviera di Oriente," and the other, "Riviera di Ponente." In California the climate of the seaboard is adequate despite its orientation, and this is also true of the Crimean Riviera around Yalta and of the westward-looking Riviera around Sochi in the Caucasus. In Florida there are no mountains, but the Everglades provide another kind of amenity. Another Riviera may be shaping on the Gulf coast of Texas with San Antonio and even Houston. Airconditioning and other gimmicks may counterbalance some unpleasant climatic features. Along the foot of the Front Ranges, Colorado is developing something that may become an inland "Riviera," where some dams and bulldozing may provide water spaces.

The same technology that frees the worker from the hardships of toiling most of his life to produce the necessities of life is also making it possible to install amenities artificially, where nature itself has not provided well enough for them. If, as some economists believe, space becomes *fungible* almost like money and securities, and one location can easily be exchanged for another, this is also true to some extent for what makes a place beautiful, exciting, and fashionable, and therefore attractive to many.

One cannot expect to decentralize and scatter so easily the places of work of the major centers of present quaternary activities; but as the volume and congestion of the great centers of "megalopolitan" character increase, some delegation of authority and deconcentration will occur, chiefly toward some centers in rapidly growing areas. Those that achieve a "Riviera-type" status will usually stand a better chance to win awards in the national and international competition. And through such a process urban life will acquire a much better quality.

There is little doubt that modern advanced societies have the means to afford the needed planning and redevelopment. There is also evidence that the forces already at play on the economic and social scene will gain more momentum in the immediate future. The percentage of the aged population, retiring with sufficient means to select a pleasant place to live, is rapidly increasing in the total population. The number of young adults, who have completed their school years and do not yet have children, and are therefore particularly mobile, selective, and looking for excitement, will increase more rapidly than any other sector of the age pyramid in the next ten years, in the countries that experienced the baby boom after 1945. Cities in America and Western Europe should prepare themselves for the impact of these waves of demanding customers. The illusion that they may all be dispersed along great new highways with more television and other gadgets ought to be dispelled. Modern people are gregarious. When they leave on vacation, with a free choice of where to go, they do not scatter in solitude amid the vast open, quiet spaces that still abound even on well-developed continents. Most congregate in a few fashionable, well-advertised, very crowded spots. This ought to be kept in mind when planning for an urban life that people will look for.

NOTES

1. "Message from the President of the United States relative to the problems and future of the central city and its suburbs," March 2, 1965, *89th Congress, 1st Session, House of Representatives, Document No. 99;* quotation from Aristotle, p. 2.
2. See Jean Gottmann, *Megalopolis, the Urbanization of the Northeastern Seaboard of the United States* (New York: The Twentieth Century Fund, 1961).
3. Statistics from the U. S. Bureau of the Census, *Statistical Abstract of the United States 1964* (85th ed.; Washington, D.C. 1964).

4. *Ibid.*, Tables 7 and 33.
5. As it has been called by geographers, beginning with Edward Ullmann of the University of Washington, and James Parsons of Berkeley.
6. See Jean Gottmann, *Megalopolis,* especially the chapters on "Commercial Organization" and "The White Collar Revolution." The figures in the preceding paragraph are from the *Statistical Abstract of the United States,* or calculated from it.

5 *The Shape of the Future*

PAUL N. YLVISAKER

Now a professor in the Woodrow Wilson School of Public and International Affairs at Princeton University after eight years as head of the public affairs program of the Ford Foundation and several years as Director of Community Affairs in New Jersey, Paul Ylvisaker sees the historic image of the city disappearing. In its place, he argues, is emerging a "national urban culture" that will be very much like what is now called Suburbia—widely dispersed but allowing within it for the economic, cultural, and political functions once thought of as necessarily confined to the densely populated, centralized cities

The next generation—accelerating the work of the present—will all but obliterate the historic image of the City, and complete the metamorphosis by which a radically new urban creature is being evolved.

What shape the future will give to this new form of urban life has already become visible enough to describe with some assurance. What it will do to the substance of urban life, and how that in turn will shape the human beings who live it, I can only guess. My guess will be no better than the hunches I go on when raising my own children to live in this future. Often these hunches go awry, and more often than not, my advice is argued down. But my children—and the urban future of which we're also parents

From a lecture, "The Shape of Future Urban Life" delivered at the New School for Social Research, October 26, 1961. Reprinted by permission of the author.

—will probably be the fonder of the Old Man for trying. At least they will know he cared; and what's more lovable, he was usually wrong.

In that mood of gaily bringing up father, permit me my parental share of fallible prophecy and unheeded advice.

This is the City that is being obliterated:

(1) The City of unrelieved residential density, distinguishable boundaries, and slow-changing form;

(2) The City capable of being defined and governed by a single and static plan.

What the future is creating is:

(1) A national urban culture, spreading amoeba-like over open land, plastic—seemingly shapeless—in its form, fluid at its boundaries, and in its cellular structure capable of infinite reproduction.

(2) An urban way of life so intricate in its design and interdependencies that it will be extremely resistant and in some respects immune to frontal efforts to plan and order it.

This is an esoteric set of propositions to have to explain, let alone defend. They relate to the outer and inner dimensions of urban life, the physical shell and the essential character. Let me begin with the easier and more obvious: the radical change in urban form which the emerging future is building around us.

This metamorphosis began when technology and steadily rising income broke the constraining force of distance, crumbled the walls of the historic City, and deposited the City's substance upon the surrounding open land.*

With inhibiting nostalgia, we have called the resulting form Suburbia, implying that we think metamorphosis is reversible and suggesting a dependence on the City of the Past which does not or will not for long exist. There is very little "sub" about this new urbia; it's the prototype of the urban form which will dominate the life of our children.

Difficult as it may be for a Manhattanite to accept (and I'll re-

* That's the way a biologist might put it; a mathematician would date the change from the time we began doubling our urban population while halving our urban densities.

lent in a moment to say why he may never fully have to) the areas of new urban growth do not inherently need much or many of what we call the downtown. At this early stage of development, yes. But less and less. Already, the population of the new growth areas has a numerical and political edge over the old city. The margin will grow rapidly, and when agriculture finally loses its control over state governments, the mantle will fall on the children of Sprawl.

Politically, not sub-urbia but super-urbia. It is the central city that becomes subordinate; no longer the matriarch, but the aging and dependent mother in the new urban household.

Not only politically but economially. . . . There is still a vital symbiotic relationship between central business district and the periphery. But it will not be long before the new growth areas—these first and second generation disciples of the Los Angeles doctrine of how to develop, despoil (choose your own word) open land—will learn how to replicate most if not all the traditionally unique advantages of the old urban core. Every year, whole chunks of the central city's uniquenesses are being pulled into the periphery by the centrifugal processes of suburban invention. Incubating enterprises can flourish elsewhere than in the downtown lofts; look for them now in university professors' garages a hundred miles out, or in the pleasant shades of those new monasteries of the mind called research and development laboratories, which have retreated to the gracious solace of the Stanfords, the Princetons, the Chapel Hills of the far countryside. The fascinations and tribulations of commuter rail traffic are leaping headlines to those who still make the long haul from main line suburbs to the downtown; but these are a dwindling few compared to those who live and work beyond the boundaries of the old city. These latter travel to work by bits and pieces of major and minor roadway, not going to, nor coming from, but round and outside and at right angles to the older city. They couldn't care less when the rails and their riders cry ouch.

The cultural role and dominance of the old city? Manhattan, yes. But even then I wonder how far off Broadway the theatre of the future is likely to migrate. Shakespeare has by now reached

Connecticut; Philadelphia's outside citizens, at least in the summer, already have ten times as many places to watch plays in the suburbs as they do downtown; and thanks to TV, the Play-of-the-Week decentralized more drama in two years than Manhattan had concentrated in twice that time.

This sounds like a savage attack on the Old City and a romance with the new. It is not. It is a statement of developing fact that most of the U.S. already knows, lives with and seems to prefer. But recognition of the fact has strangely been missing in the world of city planning. Why? Quite simply because those whose attachments are to the old order are the ones who have done most of the hiring of planners and most of the writing on urban problems: central business districts in decline; urban universities caught in the deteriorating gray areas; mayors plagued by a dwindling tax base; real estate operators crying a departing market; urban historians mourning a lost civilization.

Understandably, these partisans of the Old Order have resorted to hope. But hope alone makes a poor program of action, especially when it fails to accord with fact. The fact is, people are not going to return to the Old City in the numbers they have left; nor are industries; nor are shopping facilities; nor are commuters; nor none of the lost departed. The reasons for their going are too basic to be erased by a wish and a prayer. In the case of industry seeking land for horizontal layout and plant expansion, these reasons proceed from physical necessity; in the case of people searching for modern housing, elbow-room and freedom of choice, these reasons proceed from virtue; in the case of service establishments seeking a market, these reasons make good economics.

What in the long run is there to staunch this hemorrhaging of the old city? Not much. The supply of urbanizable land in the U.S. is so large that to this next generation it might as well be infinite. Automotive and air transportation make every part of this continent accessible; even if you are emotionally tied to Manhattan, you don't have to live there; from the Midwest, from California, from Florida, it's only a quick jet ride away. Within the present embrace of existing metropolitan areas—in the pockets of land which have been leapfrogged by the first rush of the bulldozer—there is at least another generation's space for ranch-house development.

On the drafting broads of new technology, there is at least another generation's propulsion toward the metropolitan periphery and the open space beyond. None of the new gadgetry or product development I know of is designed to reinstate the dense living patterns of the older city; electronics have a built-in penchant for urban expanse. Even Professor Vernon's concentrated world of the face-to-face is being plucked at by centrifugal forces; an Ad man I live with in the rural interior of New Jersey has cut his ties with Madison Avenue to the minimum of a couple of weekly visits—thanks to an electronic device clipped to his belt, he can potter in his garden while awaiting the unpredictable and unscheduled call which economists have told us would chain him physically to the downtown.

And in the minds of men, there is at least a generation more of the deep urge to flee the old city. Its housing is obsolescent and expensive to maintain; the new apartments are either too high in price or too low in status; you can get culture a lot more cheaply and conveniently by television than you can on Broadway; and the stigma of the slum is a dark shadow that will haunt and drive at least another generation of Whites and Negroes alike to the symbolic sanctuary of open land.

Not to mention the matter of defense. To the extent anyone is taking this matter seriously, the logic of dispersal is compelling. The old city is too easy a target.

Crying the demise of the centralized city in the midst of a booming Manhattan may seem foolhardy; I still think the prediction is accurate. We will spill out onto the land for another generation at least. Manhattan will survive longer than most; an exception, but a changing and misleading one. Already its downtown is an island of the old order in a flooding sea of the new; it is a Potemkin Village which obscures the view of the gray and green realities immediately beyond. It is not a model for the core cities of our 200 metropolitan areas; it is more a rival, siphoning off much of the economic and social potential of the Philadelphias, the Bostons, and even the Chicagos. It is sustained by the very forces that are contributing to urban dispersion throughout the country.

I would pause in this argument to concede that our society is not yet ready to accept this imminent future gladly as its permanent urban environment. Like Hamlet, we are soliloquizing—mournfully but still impotently—while events move swiftly on and around us. To be or not to be a sprawled urban civilization . . . to debate but not to decide.

I sense that as a nation—not merely as Manhattanites—we are uncertain to the point of bad conscience over having bowed thus far to the powerful forces of dispersion. Sprawl is a bad word in just about everyone's dictionary; so is suburbia; and significantly, no one has come forward to suggest a favorable name for the urban developments lately taking place. Even among the emerging majority of people who have chosen this new form, you won't find many rising publicly to boast about it. It's like being newly rich—it may feel good but it doesn't look good. These days, a Book-of-the-Month Club's circulation and income automatically awaits the author who makes a public confessional about the crack in the picture window. . . .

Arguing from analogy, one could make a persuasive case for the conservative point of view that in destroying the historic city at present speed we are recklessly uncoiling the mainspring of our civilization and dissipating the compressed power of the City aimlessly over an unready countryside.

But I don't think either the analogy or our soliloquy is influencing events; as in the case of Hamlet, our inability to decide and our unwillingness to leave the injured spirit of the past is making us even more certainly the victim of the present and inviting the worst consequences of an unsettled future. . . .

Beyond generalities, there are two specifics which need doing: One is a thought job. The City has not just grown bigger than its boundaries—it has outgrown the concept and vocabulary of the city itself. The distinction, at least in this country, has been blotted out between agricultural and urban life; television, the automobile, and the agricultural revolution have taken care of that.

Geographical distinctions are also fading; what we call the City today is to all intents and purposes the same as the nation. And in another generation or two—if we can survive the savagery of this latter-day and I think last-ditch stand of nationalism—urban society will dissolve into world society.

But each of these fading separatenesses is still being dealt with on separate assumptions and policy criteria. It shows in both our academic and real-world behavior; one of the obsolescences most relevant here is the separate way we go about national planning and urban planning. One is largely economic; the other largely physical. Neither translates very well into the other's language. Economists deal with orderly aggregates, which somehow never achieve the reality of urban form; and as I've tried to point out earlier, urban form and policy never quite seem to survive the tests of national aggregates.

It's about time we did try at least to develop a unified field theory. I'm not very hopeful that we'll ever achieve one; after all, our physical scientists aren't doing so well on that one either. But the search, with the confrontation of methods, assumptions and objectives, is one that might help narrow the rate of our urban lag. . . .

6 Notes on Southern California

NATHAN GLAZER

In this sociological travelogue, Nathan Glazer, now Professor of Education and Social Structure at Harvard University, describes Southern California and the culture it has produced. Despite occasional blemishes and deficiencies, he finds its decentralization, mobility, and new styles of life "a reasonable suggestion of how things can be" in the urban society of the future.

When I left Los Angeles one day last February, after a week in Southern California, the newspaper I picked up at the airport reported that the population of Los Angeles County was now 5,800,000, and that it would reach some unimaginable figure by 1975. I also picked up at the airport a report of the Air Pollution Control, District of the County of Los Angeles, discussing the war against smog, and you could, if you wished, put these two things together and ominously conclude that the Southern California boom was coming to an end, strangled by the very things that brought it into being. The balmy weather between the mountains and the sea now helps to create the "atmosphere inversion" that traps the smog-producing irritants. The oil which supplied a good deal of the region's first wealth is now the source of great quantities of the poisonous substances found in the atmosphere. The open space and long beaches suggested a new style of life based on the automobile, and exhaust pipes of automobiles now contribute their share of fumes to the smog. A new city, almost without traditions, growing up in the age of the automobile, suggested an urban style that permitted people to live anywhere, and thus prevented the creation of a dense city center which might support a public transportation system and reduce dependence on automobiles.

All these things are so easy to say, and two years ago, after my first trip to Southern California, I would perhaps have said them and stopped there. One's bias in favor of traditional cities —Paris, London, New York—is great, and to see Los Angeles now struggling with its very special problems may afford some malicious satisfaction. But even then, on my earlier visit, there were other things to see which might have modified this too-neat picture of the most American city being destroyed by the most American product. You could (shamefacedly) be exhilarated by the long stretches of white concrete roadway, heavily traveled at a rate of speed and with a precision and articulation in moving together and making turns that was surprising to Eastern eyes. Then there were the wild hills and mountains, almost in the middle of the city, with houses perched on top of them commanding a breathtaking view, and the buildings along Wilshire Boulevard, rather bolder in style and color than you saw in the East, but blending into something that was exciting and perhaps beautiful. One part of Los Angeles reminded you of those desolate stretches of Long Island: long roads, partly developed small-house districts, nondescript business establishments along the roadsides; other parts reminded you of a World's Fair, too extreme in its modernity and shock-impact to be taken seriously. But what separated it from Long Island was that you know, from the heavier traffic, the brighter and more ingenious neon signs, the richer gardens, that this was not a backwater, something left behind, with a city somewhere in the distance that was the real thing; this was the thing itself. The traffic, and the parking spaces around everything, meant that you could, and did, get to whatever was exciting or important or interesting. And what separated it from a World's Fair was that the sense of hectic movement and activity was here to stay, and people were living in it as a regular thing.

And then you realized: there was so much activity, so much life, so much acceptance of and pleasure in this kind of life, that you could not simply turn up your nose, and rush off to San Francisco—which is certainly prettier and pleasanter, but where there is much less building going on, and where the restaurants vie with each other to achieve a more 1890's look. You at least had to look into Los Angeles, move into the traffic, onto the freeways, head toward the beaches and the mountains, and try to feel what the millions living in Southern California, and the millions more coming, were gaining, and losing.

San Diego

The city of San Diego is about 120 miles southeast of Los Angeles. It advertises itself as smog-free. It already has more than a half million people (there were only 200,000 in 1940), it is one of the fastest growing cities in the country, and it is, in some ways, more typical of Southern California than Los Angeles. It is perhaps a good place to start with.

It has wonderful beaches, a dry, sunny climate, and a magnificent view of harbors and islands from its main downtown hotel. Hills rise behind the city, but unfortunately they aren't steep enough to provide the views one finds in Los Angeles or the San Francisco bay area. San Diego looks different from other cities and it takes a while to realize that one of the reasons it looks different is that it is rich, but rich in a new and special way. You aren't struck by the splendid houses and hotels, expensive restaurants, and other evidences of wealth—even though it has enough of these. You are struck rather by the fact that it is rich communally. To begin with, San Diego seems to command all the resources needed by a city which must lay out vast sums for the roads and parking places required by a motorized populace. You find magnificent roads paralleled by even more magnificent roads; the roadside buildings are handsome drive-ins or elegant motels, decorated with redwood, tropical plants, swimming pools, and set off by ingenious landscaping; the hills are green —thanks to expensive irrigation water; the schools brand-new with all the space in the world; the residential developments have intensively planted, well-kept gardens; there are city parks and state parks and beach parks, all well equipped; and even the used-car lots and automobile salesrooms, generally making the dreariest part of an American city, strike one as neat and clean, with their advertising signs a bit brighter and more imaginative than elsewhere. Certainly the light contributes to this effect—it is brighter and whiter than elsewhere; certainly one's being a tourist contributes to it, too. It is a tourist's reaction to see roads, and roadsides, first. But here it is also a native's reaction—they too see a good deal of the world from a car.

There is this wealth of visible, tangible things. But they are things that everyone, or almost everyone, uses: roads and parking space, motels, and drive-ins, small houses and gardens, beaches and parks, schools and government buildings. You wonder if all these roads are necessary; does this fine road need another, finer one alongside it? And if it isn't that necessary, who is paying for it? And then you come to one reason for these communal riches: San Diego is also a great naval base, and Southern California the setting for a great concentration of military bases. The entire region therefore benefits from the lavish expenditures of a wealthy government, in an area—defense—in which expenditure is always freest. So let there be yet another road, going, it appears, nowhere through empty and unusable country —but then one notices that this road is a way of getting to some air base or rocket installation, even though an unnecessarily expensive way of getting there.

The Federal government contributes more than roads to Southern California. It contributes the water by its irrigation works; it helps to provide cheap electricity with its great dams, and cheap electricity keeps things cleaner, signs brighter, and leads to the widespread phenomenon of stores being lit up all night—all adding to the festive air. In the city itself, on a group of islands in a bay, and on the surrounding shores, a great park is being developed—one reads, "By the City of San Diego in co-operation with the Army Corps of Engineers." The servicemen need parks, beaches, seaside facilities for their families—and the government helps pay for at least a good part of it.

Even culture is provided. In Balboa Park, in the middle of San Diego, is a huge complex of exposition buildings, one group in a rich Spanish Colonial style of architecture, another group, more recent, in more modern style. How is it possible for such a city, one asks, simply to maintain all these buildings, with their beautiful landscaping and wonderful gardens? The answer is, that there have been two expositions in San Diego—and the Federal government paid for the buildings and landscaping, or a good part thereof. And so San Diego is endowed with a wealth of facilities: with two large open air theaters (one surrounding a huge organ, one in a natural bowl), a large civic auditorium, a recital hall, buildings for an art gallery, a natural history museum and an anthropological museum, a replica of an Elizabethan theater in which a local group puts on plays, and other facilities too numerous to mention, but all of which seem far, far more than even a city of a half million can use. In any case, it is certainly more than it could have created from its own resources.

The help given by the Federal government is supplemented by private philanthropy. The outdoor organ is the Spreckels organ; one of the largest buildings is Ford Hall; the fine American Indian exhibits in one of the museums bear the name of Scripps, as does the Institute of Oceanography and the Art Gallery and Library of La Jolla, just to the north.

The government and the wealthy have contributed water, roads, institutions, buildings. And now it is all there, part of a concentration of communal wealth that is almost unequaled in the world.

TASTE

When you speak of Southern California taste, you think of the ice-cream parlor in the shape of an ice-cream cone, the hot-dog stand in the shape of a hot dog. But our images are always ten or twenty years behind the reality. A clean, simple line prevails in Southern California, enlivened by color in materials, by tasteful landscaping, and interesting patterns in wood—exuberance is now generally limited to the gardens and the planing. The new building is much better and bolder than the old—as compared with much of the rest of the country, where the new building is often worse than the old. The best buildings tend to be the public ones—the schools and colleges and universities, the motels and shopping centers.

Where, you wonder, did this new California taste come from? There was no tradition to follow. Of course the impact of modern architecture has been enormous, here as elsewhere, and seems to have produced a special local variant. (Compare the Wilshire Boulevard office buildings with the New York office buildings.) But then it dawns on one: the roads must have had something to do with it. They are a dominating experience, the only large common experience that could be responsible for the general upgrading of taste in Southern California. The new roads present not only simple and subtle lines, impressive cross-overs with intriguing concrete support structures and elegant curves, but they present also a clean, uncluttered landscape with continually varied shapes, colors, patterns. There are brown and green hills, there seaside cliffs, here meadows, there a strange strewing of boulders across hilly country. And on the whole, the way that Southern California is now being built up prevents the landscape from being quite as corrupted by roadside trash as was the case in the 20's and 30's. There are neat if uninspired government installations, sometimes an impressive group of buildings of a great commercial farm, the more exuberant commercial structures. The roads provide quite a different experience and image from those of the first decades of the motor age. They are probably the one uncorrupted expression of a functional-engineering outlook which most Americans regularly experience.

But throughout you are struck by an improvement in taste: it would appear that wealth alone upgrades taste. For if one compares the American roadside of the 20's and 30's with that of the

50's, or with the Mexican roadside just south of the border, you see the effect of professional signs as against crude lettering, of new, smooth surfaces as against patched, broken surfaces put together of clashing materials. Wealth may corrupt taste under certain circumstances, but after a certain point, after all traditional values and proportions have disappeared (as in lower California, and the Southern California of the 20's), wealth serves to upgrade it—somewhat.

There are of course other influences on taste besides the influence of wealth operating in a society where traditional standards have disappeared. Another influence is the very lack of a "tradition" (except for the weak Spanish one), which has left the field wide open to the homemaking and "California living" magazines. And on these we see the impact of the general rise of taste in the country, and of the victory of variants of a modern approach in architecture and design. And then another influence perhaps comes from the Japanese gardeners, who are responsible for most of the Southern California gardens. These, it is true, have at first glance little in common with Japanese gardens: they are based on the intensive cultivation of small plots, and on the availability of exotic tropical plants—two circumstances which are quite different from those that prevail in Japan. And yet the general character of these exquisite gardens probably reflects the good taste of the Japanese.

THE UNIVERSITY

Just north of San Diego, and continuous with it, along a curving seacoast with mountains looming up behind, is La Jolla. The seashore has low cliffs, fringe beaches, interesting rock formations. There are motels and apartment houses on the side nearer San Diego, and then pretty and expensive houses in pastel colors on quiet streets, and then a town center with expensive shops, tea-roomy restaurants, a library, a school, an art museum; palm trees line the streets. You think, the Riviera cannot be nicer: hardly anything on any American coastline compares with it.

And yet here the University of California has bought a tract of land and plans to build a huge new campus that in time will be as big as Berkeley and the University of California in Los Angeles, and that may be as distinguished.

This is perhaps the most striking introduction to democracy in California: that the free state university takes for a new campus (and can afford to take) some of the best and most desirable land in the state. And this, too, in a state which, because so much of it is desert, mountain, and agricultural valley, does not really have a great supply of good residential land. Nevertheless, the university moves into an exclusive seaside resort and will in time bring in thousands of poor students—who will certainly change La Jolla—and thousands of not-so-rich employees and faculty members—who will change it even more.

A Jew cannot buy a house in La Jolla today: so I was told in San Diego, where it was reported to me that even the son of a Federal judge had been unsuccessful in trying to purchase there. But what will happen to La Jolla when hundreds and then thousands of faculty members pour in, with tens and hundreds of Jews among them? Then La Jolla's little prejudices will be helplessly swept aside.

There is at present another growing campus of the university on another magnificent California coastline, near another elegant town, Santa Barbara. Another great campus will be built in the Monterey-Carmel region, one of the most beautiful coastal areas in the state, and one of its most important tourist attractions, with many expensive houses and much desirable real estate. But nothing is to too good for the University of California—the best faculty, the most expensive buildings, the best sites in the state. Before long it is expected there will be 100,000 students at its various campuses.

If you strike inland from La Jolla, taking a somewhat longer route to Los Angeles, you go through deserted, rolling country, with some good farms, and through strange, foothill country, and eventually you come out onto a great agricultural plain, the citrus-growing area which stretches westward to Los Angeles and beyond. There on the plain, up against the hills, lies yet another campus of the University of California—Riverside. Handsome, low, prairie-style brick buildings begin to outline a new campus (it is only a few years old) which is to be kept small, and which is to concentrate on a liberal arts education in a setting similar to that of small colleges in New England and the Midwest. But this small college already has resources that those other small colleges can often hardly touch: just because it is free and supported by public wealth, while they are expensive and must be supported by private donations. I walked through the open-stack library at Riverside and thought of the library that is being put up after years of painful effort at the small New England college where I was then teaching. This library had been created overnight, and yet it already surpassed that other one. It had complete series of many important scholarly and academic periodicals, it received almost every periodical one would want to look at, it had pleasant outdoor readings areas and great numbers of new books.

Los Angeles

You then proceed through Riverside itself, a pleasant town of old trees, white-painted wooden houses, and a movie theater that was showing *Open City* when I passed through. The traffic now begins to get heavier, the roads begin to widen, and you are soon approaching Los Angeles.

Finally you are on an elevated road that carries five lanes of traffic each way, and that approaches other great roads carrying the same incredible load of traffic. To enter Los Angeles on the freeway from the west, and to see the other freeways coming in, crossing over each other, with enormous rivers of cars moving from one artery to another—this is an amazing sight. What wealth has been poured into the Los Angeles freeways! How many hundreds of millions are yet to be spent upon them! From one perspective, this is a huge, misguided undertaking, a great waste of resources which might have been used for an efficient public transportation system. But it also helps make possible a life in which everyone chooses his time to come and his time to go, in which people can swim in the afternoon, work at night, and shop in huge supermarkets in the early morning, in which only a small proportion of the population of a huge metropolitan area ever sees, or has cause to see, the downtown region, in which everything can be done from a car, and in which the New Yorker, to whom a car is a torment, discovers the efficiency of being in a city in which every house, store, institution is surrounded by its own parking space. Here you can conduct your business, go to restaurants and movies, visit friends, on your own schedule. An enormous expanse of space, capital equipment, gasoline is required. But you think too that the world can probably support one great city of this type, and in any case only one country has the resources and the land to carry through such a utopian enterprise. Utopian it is, because a city of this type demands that every adult has his own car—and Los Angeles is not very far from that now. Yet still the traffic moves, and more rapidly than in New York.

But finally you get off the freeway to descend into an endless Brooklyn or Queens: single-family houses, stretching for mile upon mile, with occasional streets devoted to business. But with this difference from Brooklyn or Queens: that here everyone has chosen his way of life, while Brooklyn and Queens have not been chosen, but taken out of necessity. The sense of a chosen city, a desired way of life, a realized wish, is strong. We should not be deceived by the surface resemblance to the endless "bedroom boroughs" of New York and Chicago. Here the bedroom and living room are mixed. The streets with little houses are as busy with traffic as great thoroughfares in the East. This may offend our sense of the proper organization of a city, but in any case the curse of the bedroom is removed when it is not separated from the city by a long ride, at the same hour each day, by subway, trains, or bus. Here the city is scattered all around, as if a bomb had distributed Manhattan south of 59th Street homogeneously throughout Brooklyn, Queens, and the Bronx.

The People

There are of course the old people who have retired, and moved in hundreds of thousands from the Midwest and South. Nathanael West's *The Day of the Locust* described them with horror, and fixes the image of Los Angeles as a place of horror. And yet you don't see these people: they are not on Wilshire Boulevard or in Hollywood, or Beverly Hills, or Westwood, or Fairfax, or in the Valley, or in Boyle Heights, or on Adams and Jefferson Boulevard. Perhaps there are fewer of them than there used to be: they are in any case less mobile and certainly less visible than other parts of the Los Angeles population. More visible are hundreds of thousands of Mexicans, and hundreds of Negroes. Despite the tight-lipped oldsters from the Midwest and the South, Los Angeles is quite an enlightened city: not as enlightened as San Francisco and New York, but not far behind them.

It is the second largest Jewish city in the country—there are 400,000 Jews or more. There are 40,000 Japanese, more than before the wartime relocation, which uprooted thousands from farms. The old concentration of these groups in downtown Los Angeles has been broken up, by relocation and then by the vast postwar freeway building which has wiped out large areas in the downtown section that were Negro, Mexican, Japanese, and Jewish. This downtown destruction has been combined with vast building on the outskirts: and so the Negroes and Mexicans and Japanese and poor Jews can find fairly good housing (by that I mean—better than in other cities in which they live) that has been left behind by other groups moving out, and we find Negroes, and Mexicans, and Jews, and Japanese, or two or three of these groups, living amicably together in many neighborhoods.

The main Japanese neighborhood has now moved to the west, and stretches for perhaps a mile or so along West Jefferson, and reaches back into surrounding streets. It blends into a Negro neighborhood to the east, and is itself mixed most of the way. You see large and prosperous stores run by Japanese, you see a score of real estate offices—advertising investment property, which seems to be favored by the group. You see a well-designed supermarket with attached one-story offices (a common California arrangement—everyone thus has parking space)—and they contain the offices of a Japanese architect, accountant, lawyer, doctor, dentist. You know too that from this neighborhood and others come great numbers of students for the University of California in Los Angeles—1,000 Japanese attend the university, I was told.

And then there are the young people. So many American cities lose them, so few attract them. Los Angeles is one of those that still attracts them. It is far away, it is different, there are jobs, some of them interesting and glamorous. You suspect that Hollywood's declining predominance in the entertainment industry has been accompanied not only by a rise in its taste, but a rise in the level and character of young people that it and the related entertainment industries attract. You wonder whether Hollywood twenty years ago could have provided the people to support so many little theaters, coffeehouses, and other gathering places for young people of artistic and intellectual bent. In any case, Los Angeles today, with New York and San Francisco, has a "Village"—a place with little theaters (more than one) and coffeehouses, small night clubs in which you hear folk singers, psychoanalytically-wise comedians, flamenco guitarists, and such. Whatever the meaning of all this for the history of culture (and it may be a curse, conceivably), for a city it is fun, and you can hardly imagine a great city without its bohemia. Los Angeles qualifies; its bohemia is different in quality, perhaps inferior in quality, to that of San Francisco, as that is perhaps inferior to New York's. But its differences also make it interesting. The three bohemias sort out, from the young people coming from the towns and cities of the country, and from these three cities themselves, somewhat different types. Some people, of course, try all three.

Bohemia, too, is democratic: and in a party on the Hollywood hills you will find people who will want to act and people who have actually been seen on the screen, a nightclub chef (his working hours are the same as the entertainers, and he knows them), a jewelry salesman, a psychiatrist from New York for a medical convention, people who are quite indefinable, and a visiting intellectual from New York. The house is an expensive one, but the party is being held in a kind of basement room in which a poor hopeful actor lives, built into the hill, and opening on a garden with a swimming pool, and there is a fine view of the city —for it is winter, and the winds have blown the smog away.

Work

Los Angeles looks less like a place where people work than any other great city in the world. There are no busy skyscrapers filled with office workers and garment workers, as in New York. The tallest buildings in the city are some downtown government buildings, some elegant hotels, the Prudential Life Insurance Company on Wilshire Boulevard, the Angelus and Mormon temples. There are oil wells and refineries—but they require few workers. The movies and television are main industries, and you do see huge studios—but that is not exactly one's typical image of work. There are factories—but they make things like airplanes and electronic equipment, which require no belching smokestacks. There is no surge of workers into and out of the city—the traffic is dense morning and evening, but it is going both ways, and you can't be sure who is going to the beach, the supermarket, Disneyland, or to work.

Indeed, the gap between work and play in Los Angeles must be narrower than in any other great city. Where do people work in Los Angeles? In supermarkets, in gasoline stations, in parking lots, in the movies, in hotels and motels and restaurants, as gardeners, in offices which have tropical plants and bright cars right outside the door, outdoors as building workers, indoors in bright new factories. And the same universal vehicle, the car, serves work and pleasure interchangeably, and the vast complex of economic activities which serve the car also serve work and pleasure interchangeably.

Life is hard and life is earnest, and there are coal miners and steelworkers and auto workers and textile mill operatives—but not in Los Angeles. There freer styles of work prevail, operating in an urban environment which is more successful in obscuring the sharp division between work and nonwork than any other. There are the backyard swimming pools and the beaches, which can be used three-quarters of the year, there is the huge array of service jobs which can be worked at part-time and at odd hours and on odd days, there are all the nonworking people who have come with a little money and invested in real estate, and those who have come with nothing but live on pensions. More people act as if they were on vacation (and must feel it, too) than anywhere in the world. There is no way of telling it is Sunday in Los Angeles unless one looks at the calendar.

Los Angeles produces less than any other great city of the things that, from a grim, Protestant way of looking at things, anyone really *needs.* And yet it grows like mad. And those other cities, that supply the country with useful things like coal and steel and cloth and machinery, decline. For Los Angeles, everything has been made easy. The vast investment that is required to maintain 6,000,000 people and 3,000,000 automobiles in the desert seems to require little effort from anyone. The water and the electricity come from hundreds of miles away, and the government helped to pay for it anyway. The oil only has to be taken from the ground. The cars come from Detroit. The roads are paid for by the government, or the gasoline tax. And the complicated engineering effort needed to do all these things only requires money and engineers, and there is plenty of both. There is the smog—but that too can be solved by money and engineers. It is hard to see how the machine can stop, and leave these people without water for the gardens, electricity for the bright lights, cars to run around in.

All the rhythms in Los Angeles are different—the daily movement in and out of the city center is hardly greater than other movements, the weekly cycle is scarcely noticeable, the seasonal cycle is different. That dividing line between work and nonwork that is at the basis of so much of Western achievement, and misery, loses its sharpness. But perhaps for our society in general work has already done its job, and we can keep things going with much less of it. And if we can, Southern California is not an aberration, but a reasonable suggestion as to how things can be.

7

The Metropolitan Area as a Racial Problem

MORTON GRODZINS

Many of the efforts to describe or plan the future of urban areas pay little attention to the racial composition of the urban and suburban populations. As the late Morton Grodzins, Professor of Political Science at the University of Chicago, pointed out in this prescient essay written in 1957, the massive migration of black Americans to the cities will inevitably affect their future form and character. The population trends he describes have continued and the problems he identifies have become more acute. There is little evidence yet of either sufficient understanding to devise effective solutions to these problems or of sufficient will to take those measures that might be necessary. Yet, as Grodzins points out, the character of American cities in the future will necessarily be affected by how the problems created by their changing racial character are dealt with.

Almost nothing is being done today to meet what is likely to be the nation's most pressing social problem tomorrow. The problem can be stated in all its bleakness: many central cities of the great metropolitan areas of the United States are fast becoming lower class, largely Negro slums.

The Great Schism of Population

. . . For several decades the Negro population of the great cities has been increasing more rapidly than the white population. The great changes come in time of full employment, and the ex-

Pittsburgh: University of Pittsburgh Press, 1957. Reprinted by permission of the University of Pittsburgh Press.

plosive growth, as measured by the decennial censuses, took place between 1940 and 1950. In that decade, the total population of the fourteen largest metropolitan areas increased by 19 per cent, the total Negro percentage gain (65.1 per cent) being more than four times greater than the white increase (15.6 per cent). Negroes increased proportionately more rapidly in both central cities and suburbs, but the significant growth differential was inside the great cities. . . .

As late as 1950 nonwhites constituted only a minor fraction of the total population in most of the central cities of the fourteen largest metropolitan areas. Washington, D.C., with nonwhites totalling 35.4 per cent of total population, and Baltimore (23.8 per cent) had the largest group of nonwhites in proportion to total population. In addition to these, only three other cities had 1950 Negro populations in excess of 15 per cent; three had less than 10 per cent.

Continued Negro migration, the comparatively greater rate of natural increase among nonwhites, and the exodus of whites to the suburbs will dramatically raise the proportion of nonwhites in central cities. . . .

Estimates of future population trends must take into account some reurbanization of white suburbanites as the proportion of older people increases and the suburbs become less attractive to those whose children have grown up and left home. Even making allowances for shifts of this sort, all evidence makes it highly probable that within 30 years Negroes will constitute from 25 to 50 per cent of the total population in at least 10 of the 14 largest central cities.

The suburbs of the metropolitan areas exhibit very different population trends. Negroes made up only 4 per cent of their population in 1940 and less than 5 per cent in 1950. (Central city nonwhites were 9 per cent of the total population in 1940, 13.2 per cent in 1950.) . . .

The general picture of the future is clear enough; large nonwhite concentrates (in a few cases, majorities) in the principal central cities; large white majorities, with segregated Negro enclaves in the areas outside.

Growth Patterns Within Cities

The pattern of Negro population growth within the central cities follows established and well-understood patterns. It is based upon immigration from the South, and it is accelerated by a larger rate of natural increase of the nonwhite in-migration in comparison with the older white residents. Migration has been the source of the largest increase in most nonsouthern cities, and continued industrial expansion may actually increase this movement in the years immediately ahead. The "push" from the South may grow stronger as the consequence of growing white antagonisms following attempts to enforce the Supreme Court's nonsegregation decisions. And the "pull" of the northern cities may become more forceful as the Negro communities there become larger and more firmly established and as information concerning job and other opportunities correspondingly flows back to relatives and friends. On the other hand, the relatively more rapid natural increase of Negroes, in comparison with white residents, will almost certainly become less striking with the passage of years.

The spatial expansion of Negro population in the larger cities follows roughly similar patterns. One universal rule is that residential concentrations are segregated. In every major city with a considerable number of Negroes there exists a "black belt" or a series of "black areas." In Chicago, 79 per cent of all Negroes in 1950 lived in census tracts in which at least 75 per cent of the residents were Negroes. At the opposite extreme, 84 per cent of the non-Negroes resided in census tracts in which less than 1 per cent of the residents were Negro,[1] and the disparity would be even higher if Negro servants "living in" were not counted. Chicago's segregation pattern is somewhat extreme, but all cities follow this pattern. Negroes live preponderantly or exclusively with Negroes, whites with whites.

A second rule is equally general: once an urban area begins to swing from predominant white to predominant Negro occupancy, the change is rarely reversed. Between 1920 and 1950 in Chicago there are no cases in which areas of predominantly Negro residents reverted to areas of white occupancy. More than this, a neighborhood with a substantial proportion of Negroes (say 25 per cent) rarely retains its mixed character for a considerable period of time. The Duncans, in their intensive study of neighborhood changes in Chicago, found not a single instance between 1940 and 1950 of a census tract "with mixed population (25–75 per cent nonwhite) in which succession from white to Negro occupancy was arrested"[2] though, as they remark, the succession was more rapid in some tracts than in others. Postwar programs of public housing and urban renewal have somewhat altered this rule, in some cases establishing new Negro concentrates where they had not previously existed and in others demonstrating that relatively stable interracial patterns of living can be achieved.[3] But new housing programs in predominantly Negro areas have for the most part meant the simple exchange of one Negro population group for another; and urban renewal programs, by displacing Negro families in one area, have frequently had the effect of hastening the succession of adjacent areas to all-Negro occupancy.

A third generalization is that the pattern of Negro residential expansion is from the core of the city outward. The original concentration is almost everywhere near the center of the city. It subsequently expands radially or in concentric circles. A map by zones for virtually every city with a sizeable Negro population shows higher percentages of Negro residence in areas closest to the city center with decreasing proportions as the distance from the city center increases.

A fourth generalization is also possible. The Negro population moves generally into areas already characterized by high residential mobility. Furthermore, there is a rough comparability between the social characteristics of the in-migrant Negro population and the out-migrant white population with respect to such factors as educational attainment, rate of unemployment, room crowding, home ownership, and white collar employment.[4] Lower-class Negroes, in other words, tend to move into lower-class neighborhoods; middle-class Negroes into middle-class neighborhoods. The "piling up" process—the gross overcrowding of dwellings and areas—occurs only after the transition from white to Negro dominance has taken place.

The "Tipping" Mechanism

The process by which whites of the central cities leave areas of Negro in-migration can be understood as one in the social-psychology of "tipping a neighborhood." The variations are numerous, but the theme is universal. Some white residents will not accept Negroes as neighbors under any conditions. But others, sometimes willingly as a badge of liberality, sometimes with trepidation, will not move if a relatively small number of Negroes move into the same neighborhood, the same block, or the same apartment building. Once the proportion of nonwhites exceeds the limits of the neighborhood's tolerance for interracial living (this is the "tip point"), the whites move out. The proportion of Negroes who will be accepted before the tip point is reached varies from city to city and from neighborhood to neighborhood.

The process is not the simple one of "flight" that is a part of the real estate mythology of changing neighborhoods. It may take a number of years before the "invaded" neighborhood becomes an all-Negro one. Nor is the phenomenon uniformly one in which Negroes "push" whites out. As already noted, areas of heavy Negro in-migration are most often areas already characterized by high mobility; and the process of Negroes taking up vacancies as they occur cannot be conceived as one in which the old residents have been "pushed." This is to say that tipping may come slowly and does not necessarily indicate any immediate downgrading of the given neighborhood. What it signifies is the unwillingness of white groups to live in proximity to large numbers of Negroes.

In a few areas around the country Negroes and whites live side by side without fuss or fanfare. This is true even in Chicago, where segregation patterns are extreme, and examples of "open occupancy" can be found from New York to San Francisco.[5] Furthermore, in recent years, there has been a tendency for a single Negro family—usually of considerable income and of the professions—to find a dwelling in an all-white neighborhood. In every such case of "interracial living," however, some factor—economic or other—limits the ingress of Negro residents.

Education and community organization can extend tolerance and thus increase the proportion of Negroes in a given area before the tip point is reached. But the limits have not proved to be infinitely elastic. Even where goodwill, community effort, and financing have been maximized, the psychology of tipping has operated. The only interracial communities in the United States, with the exception of some abject slums, are those where limits exist upon the influx of nonwhites.

Patterns of Suburban Exclusion

The sheer cost of suburban housing excludes Negroes from many suburban areas. Furthermore, the social satisfactions of slum or near-slum existence for a homogeneous population have been insufficiently studied, and it is undoubtedly true that many Negro urban dwellers would not easily exchange life in all-Negro big-city neighborhoods for interracial suburban homes, even if moderately priced. The crucial fact, however, is that Negroes do not have any free choice in the matter. They are excluded from suburbia by a wide variety of devices.

Social antagonisms of suburban communities are themselves effective. Where it is plainly understood that Negroes are not wanted, Negro suburbanization is for all practical purposes impossible. In addition, suburban communities use their control of zoning, subdivision, and building regulations to achieve exclusion. Minimum lot sizes are increased to two or more acres; requirements for expensive street improvements are made—and then waived only in favor of "desirable" developments; large-scale building operations are defined as "business" for zoning purposes, thus excluding the possibility of low or moderate income suburbán building; the suburb itself purchases all vacant land parcels that are large enough for subdivision and resells only to favored purchasers; builders are required to obtain certificates from the school board that educational accommodation will be adequate for the new residences; ordinances regulating "look alike" features or requiring certain building materials make home building expensive.

Where legal barriers of this sort are not sufficient to maintain a "white only" policy, land use controls are used informally—and of course illegally—to exclude Negroes. A Philadelphia builder recently told an interviewer that he would very much like to sell suburban houses to Negroes, but that it was impossible because it would ruin him economically. "If I sold just one suburban home to a Negro, the local building inspectors would have me moving pipes three-eights of an inch every afternoon in every one of the places I was building; and moving a pipe three-eights of an inch is mighty expensive if you have to do it in concrete."[6]

These practices are combined with social and economic pressures upon white owners of older homes and upon real estate brokers. Mortgage bankers habitually discriminate against the Negro buyer in the white neighborhood, and not always for purely economic reasons. Where all else fails, suburban residents have often turned to violence to prevent Negro occupancy. The total suburban facade is relatively impenetrable.

Suburban restrictions are everywhere aimed at Negroes as a racial group and not simply against people of low or moderate income. When such restrictions are applied uniformly, they of course also affect whites. But even this has an indirect effect upon the Negro concentrates within the cities. If middle- and lower-class whites who live next door to the slums were able to move to the suburbs, their places would quickly be taken by the slum-dwellers, especially those Negroes whose presence in the slums is due less to income than to the prejudice which excludes them from more desirable places. By raising the price of housing in the suburbs, land use regulations reduce the movement of the white middle and lower classes out of the city. And this in turn holds the slum-dweller in the slums and, accordingly, the Negro in the ghetto.

Consequences of Population Distribution

Some of the consequences of the urban-suburban racial and class schism are already apparent, and others can be reasonably predicted.

Social Consequences

Within the cities the first result is a spreading of slums. There is no free market for Negro housing. The Negro population always increases faster than the living space available to it. New areas that open up to the Negro residence become grossly overcrowded by conversion of one-family houses to multiple dwellings and by squeezing two or more Negro families into apartments previously occupied by a single white one. Though complete statistical evidence is lacking, it is likely that Negroes pay substantially more rent for such accommodations than do whites, and the higher rent itself produces higher densities. Housing occupied by Negroes is more crowded, more dilapidated, and more lacking in amenities such as private baths than housing occupied by whites with equivalent incomes.

Income factors account in part for the condition of life of the the Negro community. Negroes are heavily over-represented in low income jobs: in the menial services, in unskilled and semiskilled factory labor, and in "dirty work" generally. In this respect they are not unlike some earlier immigrants to the city; the Irish and the Poles, for example, also settled mainly in the slums.

Like previous newcomers to the city tasting the freedom of urban life for the first time, a significant portion of the Negro group does not possess the stable patterns of thought and action that characterize the "better" older inhabitants. And, as with all immigrant groups, old community patterns of control do not operate well in the new environment. Family disorganization among urban Negroes is high as measured by such indices as broken marriages, families headed by females, and unrelated individuals living in the same household. The development of social stabilization pivoted on family and community ties takes place against great odds. How does a mother keep her teen-age son off the streets if an entire family must eat, sleep, and live in a single room? What utility can be found in sobriety among a society of drinkers and in a block of taverns? What opportunity for quiet amidst the din of a tightly packed, restless neighborhood?

The conditions of urban life, rather than socializing new Negro residents to "desirable" life patterns, frequently have the opposite effect. They encourage rowdiness, casual and competitive sexuality, and a readiness for combat. The result is that the neighborhoods acquired by Negro residents eventually spiral downward. Disease and crime rates are high. Family stability is further prejudiced. Filth accumulates. The slum spreads outward.

These very conditions of life in the predominantly Negro neighborhoods lead the larger population to resist the expansion of Negro residential areas. The racial attribute—skin color—is added to the social attributes of lower class behavior. And while Negroes, like other urban immigrants can readily lose undesirable social attributes, they cannot lose their color. They therefore do not have the mobility of other immigrant groups. They are racially blocked, whatever their social *bona fides*.

The Negro "black belts" of the great American cities as a consequence are by no means homogeneous. The very concentration of population within them plus the visible badge of color give them a spurious air of likeness. They contain, in fact, wide ranges of every social attribute: from illiteracy to high learning, from filth to hospital-like hygienic standards, from poverty to riches, from political backwardness to sophistication. Though the casual observer of the "black belt" neighborhoods sees only slums, the fact is that in every such area there are sub-areas, frequently on the periphery of the high-density mass, that are anything but slums. These are usually neighborhoods of newest acquisition, inhabited by the well-to-do of the Negro community. Density is low, lawns and gardens are well-tended, church attendance is high, neatness and cleanliness are apparent, parental standards of propriety for children higher than for comparable white groups.

Negro neighborhoods in the shadows of white luxury apartments are not unknown; but the more usual pattern is for low-income non-Negroes to occupy a buffer zone between all-Negro and the better white neighborhoods. Some of these are themselves new migrants to the city: Southerners and Japanese-Americans in Chicago, Puerto Ricans in New York, for example. Others are old residents on the lower ends of the income scale, people who, like the Negroes themselves, do not find success in life, or life itself, easy.

With the exodus of middle and upper classes to the suburbs, lower-income groups constitute a larger and larger fraction of the population of the central cities. Members of these groups generally exhibit a greater degree of intolerance and racial prejudice than do other whites. And the increasing juxtaposing of the Negro and the low-income non-Negro populations produces increased interracial tensions. Shirley Star of the National Opinion Research Center has shown that the greatest white animosity towards Negroes is found on the edge of the expanding Negro residential areas where whites fear their block or neighborhood will soon be "invaded."[7] In these lower class and lower-middle class transitional areas, violence is incipient. Individual differences within the minority group are ignored. A young white resident of such an area in Chicago recently beat a Negro to death with a hammer. "I just wanted to get one of them," he explained, "which one didn't matter."

The total situation produces Negro communities in which people live their whole lives without, or with minimum, contact with the other race. With a Negro population numbering in the hundreds of thousands, and with this population densely concentrated, one can live, eat, shop, work, play, and die in a completely Negro community. The social isolation of the northern urban Negro is, for very large numbers, more complete than it ever was for the Negro rural resident in the South.

Even in education, the urban residential segregation of the nonsouthern cities has produced consequences that are not dissimilar to what the South is trying to maintain by the use of violence and unconstitutional law. If segregation is defined not in legal terms but in the numbers of students who attend all-Negro schools, then it is undoubtedly true that more Negro students are segregated in the schools of New York and Chicago than in any other cities or some states.

This general picture of segregation needs some qualification. A small number of church groups have succeeded in building interracial congregations. Qualified Negro workers are finding employment in places previously barred to them, not only in manufacturing, but also in the professions and in retail establishments. On a few blocks in urban America, Negroes and whites have demonstrated that they can live together as neighbors. Labor unions, though traditionally anti-Negro, have in some places accepted Negroes as full partners in leadership as well as membership.

These are evidence of advances toward social integration. Other advances have been made within the Negro community itself. As this community in a given city grows larger, satisfactory career lines, economic security, and the home and community life that accompany such developments become possible. Here, however, Negroes and whites meet each other across separate societies rather than within a single group. The Negro shares with whites the better things of life, but he does so in isolation with other Negroes. The disadvantaged segregated community even produces advantages for some individuals within it, providing protected markets for Negro professionals and businessmen and protected constituencies for Negro political and church leaders. Yet even those who profit from segregation suffer from it. They feel the pin-pricks as well as the sledges of discrimination, and they must suppress their dissatisfaction in accordance with standards of conduct expected of all "better" people, whatever their race.

The larger evidence is neither that of social integration nor of intracommunity social gains. Rather it is evidence pointing to the expansion of Negro slums within the largest cities and the separation of whites and Negroes by intra-city neighborhoods and especially on central city-suburban lines.

Economic Consequences

Population shifts bring with them major economic consequences. Of first importance is the further decline of a large segment of business activity and associated property values, in the central cities. For reasons only remotely related—or unrelated—to the Negro-white population distribution, the economic feasibility of decentralized retail shopping has already been demonstrated. Suburban shopping centers have captured a large segment of the market in clothing, furniture, and other consumption goods; almost everywhere the "downtown" shops of the central cities have lost ground, absolutely and proportionally, to the peripheral developments. Retail sales in the central business district of Chicago decreased by 5 per cent between 1948 and 1954, while sales in the metropolitan area outside the city increased by 53 per cent. The relative sales loss of downtown areas has been even greater in other central cities.

Further developments can be foreseen. The downtown stores, with nonwhite and low-income customers more and more predominant in their clientele, will tend to concentrate on cheaper merchandise. " 'Borax' for downtown, 'Herman Miller' for the suburb," is already a slogan of the furniture business. The decline of the central-city department store will be accompanied by a general deterioration of the downtown area. There are some striking exceptions, most notably in mid-town Manhattan. But in most cities—Chicago, Boston, Los Angeles are good examples—the main streets are becoming infested with sucker joints for tourists: all night jewelry auctions, bargain linens and cheap neckties, hamburger stands and jazz dives. The slums, in other words, are spreading to the central business districts.

A further, though more problematic, development is that the offices of the large corporations will join the flight from the city, taking along with them their servicing businesses: banks, law offices, advertising agencies, and others. The rapid development of closed circuit television, facsimile reproduction, and other technical aids relieves these businesses of the necessity of clustering at a central point. Their exodus from the city is already underway. New highways will make it easier in many places to get from one suburb to another than from suburb to downtown; and the losses of giving up central headquarters can be amortized over a number of years, frequently at considerable tax savings. Even the downtown hotel is likely to give way to the suburban motel except for convention purposes, an incidental further boost to the honkey-tonk development within the downtown business areas.

The rule seems to be a simple one: retail trade, the white collar shops, and the service industries will follow population. (Once their exodus is well underway, they also lead population.) The same general rule at least partially applies for manufacturing: the greatest suburbanization of manufacturing has taken place in those metropolitan areas where there has also been the most marked suburbanization of population, and some evidence indicates that manufacturing precedes population, rather than vice versa. Though the central cities have lost some manufacturing to both suburban and nonmetropolitan areas, they have nevertheless maintained the preponderant share of the nation's total manufacturing enterprise. As Kitagawa and Bogue have shown, "the over-all spatial distribution [of manufacturing] in the United States has changed comparatively little in the past 50 years."[8] The relative immobility of heavy industry has the result of fixing the laboring and semi-skilled groups, including large numbers of Negroes, within the central cities.

Even a conservative view must anticipate the exodus of a large segment of retail and other nonmanufacturing businesses from downtown centers. Abandonment of these centers will lead to a host of municipal problems, not least of which is the loss of a substantial tax base. These economic developments are at once a step towards, and a consequence of, the city-suburban bifurcation of races that promises to transform many central cities into lower class ethnic islands. Successful attempts by central cities to encourage the establishment of new manufacturing plants as a means of rebuilding their tax base will of course hasten this process.

Political Consequences

Whatever the melancholy resemblance between older segregation patterns of the rural South and newer ones of the urban North, one important fact is different: the Negroes of the North possess the suffrage. How will they use it if they become the majority group—or at least the largest single group—in some of the great cities of the nation?

The most likely political development is the organization of Negroes for ends conceived narrowly to the advantage of the Negro community. Such a political effort might aim to destroy zoning and building restrictions for the immediate purpose of enlarging opportunities for desperately needed Negro housing against stubborn social pressures. If successful, the outcome might merely extend the Negro ghetto and cause a further departure of white populations to the suburbs. Yet the short-run political appeal of this action cannot be denied.

What the Negroes seek for themselves in Chicago in 1975 or 1985 might not be any more selfishly conceived than what Irish-dominated city councils in Boston and New York have sought in the past. In one essential field, Negro leadership may be more advantageous to the whole population: lacking devotion to the parochial schools, it would not be mean in the support of public schools. The rub lies in the very visibility of Negro domination. Even on the assumption of Negro leaders and followers demonstrating wisdom and forbearance, what would be the consequence in one or more major cities of the city councils becoming predominantly Negro? What will be the situation in a state legislature when the largest group of big-city representatives are Negroes?

At the very least, cities politically dominated by Negroes will find it more difficult to bring about the urban-suburban cooperation so badly needed in so many fields. They will find greatly exacerbated what is already keenly felt in a majority of states: the conflict between the great urban center and the rural "downstate" or "upstate" areas. Similar unfortunate effects will follow in the national Congress, once a number of large cities are largely represented by Negro congressmen. The pitting of whites against Negroes, and of white policies against Negro policies, does not await actual Negro urban domination. The cry has already been raised in states legislatures. The conflict can only grow more acute as race and class become increasingly coterminous with local government boundaries.

In the long run, it is highly unlikely that the white population will allow Negroes to become dominant in the cities without resistance. The cultural and economic stakes are too high. One countermeasure will surely present itself to the suburbanites: to annex the suburbs, with their predominantly white populations, to the cities. This will be a historic reversal of the traditional suburban antipathy to annexation. But in the perception of suburbanites it will be justified: they will be annexing the city to the suburbs.

The use of annexation to curb Negro political powers is already underway. It was an explicit argument used by political leaders favoring an annexation to Nashville in 1952. And other recent annexations, largely confined to the South, have taken place at least partially to deny Negroes political powers they would otherwise achieve.

Other actions to the same end can be expected, especially the gerrymandering of Negro populations so as to deny them equitable representation in legislative bodies of city, state, and nation. Tuskegee, Alabama, was gerrymandered in 1957 to exclude all but a handful of Negro voters from city elections, and steps are currently under way to divide Macon County among five neighboring counties. Negroes have long lived within the city, and the county has for many years been preponderantly Negro, but only recently have the Negroes exercised their franchise in any numbers. In the border city of Cincinnati, fear of growing Negro political power was an important reason for the 1957 action that repealed proportional representation and subsequently defeated the reform City Charter Committee. During the campaign over proportional representation, whispering campaigns urged defeat of the system in order to prevent Theodore M. Berry, Negro vice-mayor, from becoming mayor, as well as to prevent Negroes from moving into white neighborhoods. The total political picture of continued racial bifurcation forecasts a new round of political repression aimed at Negroes. For this one, they will be better armed—effective numbers, economic strength, political sophistication, and allies in the white population.

Toward Solutions

If racial separation and segregation lead to evil consequences, the cure is obvious; the separation should be ended. For no problem is a solution more easily stated: white populations should be brought back into the central cities, and Negroes should be allowed to choose freely where they want to live in all areas of central cities and suburbs alike. No solution is more difficult to implement.

Racial exclusiveness may be conceived as an "American dilemma" in moral terms, or a Marxian problem of class antagonisms, or a Freudian expression of instinctual attractions and cultural taboos. From these perspectives the "race problem" may be solved, if at all, only through the slow marches of gradual social change. Neither laws, nor adult education, nor *ad hoc* institutional programs can be decisive.

It can certainly be assumed that for a long time for some people in some places no program of residential integration will be palatable or acceptable. Yet is is also true that people are not frozen in antagonistic attitudes, that change is possible, and that the change can best be achieved by actual successful experiences in interracial living. Most importantly, plans can be built upon the great diversity of outlook and attitude among the urban populations of mid-century America.

Creating a Free Real Estate Market

The most important general step to be taken is to remove the restrictions on where Negroes may live. This is, in the first place, an act of simple justice. Of greater relevance here, if nonwhites possessed genuine residential mobility, it would go a long way toward eliminating the great social costs of the present population distribution. From free movement, it follows that (1) there would be less overcrowding in Negro areas; (2) there would be fewer and smaller all-Negro neighborhoods; and (3) individual Negroes would self-selectively distribute themselves, as white populations do, among neighborhoods whose social characteristics are roughly homogeneous and roughly similar to their own.

It should not be supposed that the removal of restrictions would end Negro residential concentrations. Income factors alone will confine many Negroes to the least desirable residential areas for a long time to come. Considerations of sociability are also an important concentrating factor. Investments in businesses and living quarters will keep even many of those who can afford to move as residents of all-Negro areas. Yet many Negroes now live in Negro neighborhoods simply because they have no other place to go. With the occupational upgrading and increased income that Negroes are achieving in ever-growing numbers, there is no doubt that freedom to choose residences would result in a scattering of Negro families throughout the entire urban area.

That many Negroes would continue to reside in areas of all-Negro concentration, even under circumstances that permit dispersion, would, in fact, make easier the dispersion process. Only a limited number of nonwhites can afford, and wish, to move to white neighborhoods. This means that there could be a relatively complete dispersion of those so inclined, without their number becoming large in any single neighborhood.

The case of nondiscrimination housing laws can best be argued in these terms. Such laws would allow the widespread dispersion of nonwhites. Given the limited number of nonwhites who would choose in the foreseeable future to take advantage of such laws, their main impact would be in preventing the kinds of concentration that frequently turn present "open occupancy" communities into crowded all-Negro slums.

Nondiscriminatory laws, however, can do more harm than good unless they are enacted in large jurisdictions. The smallest effective area is probably a very large city. In smaller areas their effect might be to create the flight of white residents to "lily-white" jurisdictions. The full effect of nondiscriminatory laws can be felt only if, in a given region, there are no such areas to which to flee. Even under this circumstance, laws against discrimination may produce a scattering of all-Negro residential pockets rather than genuine dispersions unless attempts are made to prevent the concentration of Negroes in any given neighborhood.

Panic flights of old-resident whites at the appearance of one or a few new-resident Negro families will be discouraged if the old residents know that, no matter where they move, a similar development might take place. The new residents in most cases will seek to avoid another all-Negro neighborhood. The interests of old and new residents become congruent on the points of maintaining neighborhood standards and mixed, rather than all-Negro, occupancy. Other less happy outcomes are of course possible. But nondiscrimination laws, where combined with a sensitivity to the importance of not crowding Negroes into any single area, provide opportunities for giving Negroes the free residential choice they should have while simultaneously producing minimum disturbance in existing communities.[9]

Controlled Migration

The case for nondiscriminating laws thus rests largely on the point that they would filter nonwhites in relatively small numbers to white communities. Laws of this sort are difficult to enforce. (How does one prove discrimination if a seller decides not to sell?)

Population groups are infinitely facile in frustrating unpopular laws. Public acceptance is necessary if interracial living is to be made possible.

The tipping phenomenon has meant that interracial communities in the United States (outside some slum areas) exist only where there also exist limits on the influx of nonwhites. In the usual case, these limits have been economic in nature. Thus the

Kenwood region of Chicago is a truly interracial one. Homes in this neighborhood are large and expensive to maintain, and municipal housing codes are rigidly enforced. Pure economic pressures, combined with community acceptance of those Negroes who can afford to live there, have produced an upper-middle class interracial neighborhood.

In other cases, control of in-migration has been consciously contrived. The developers of the Philadelphia suburbs of Concord Park and Greenbelt Knoll have announced their intention of maintaining a white–Negro ratio of 55–45. Prospective purchasers place their names on a waiting list, and a purchase is made possible only if it maintains the desired racial distribution.

It is doubtful that many population groups, other than confirmed, egalitarian Quakers, would accept a ratio of Negroes at this high a point. On the other hand, Negro political leaders in the large cities could probably not remain political leaders if they were willing to accept controlled interracialism, set at a ratio that most whites would accept.

Nevertheless, experimentation with various systems of controlled migration is highly desirable. The tip-point phenomenon is so universal that it constitutes strong evidence in favor of control. Without control there has been a total failure to achieve interracial communities involving substantial numbers of Negroes anywhere in the great urban areas of America. Where controlled migration has been achieved, so has interracial living.

Many methods can be found to implement a controlled migration. A free real estate market, accompanied by enforced, adequate housing codes, is the preferred mechanism. The direct rationing of sales, as in the Philadelphia suburbs, is possible in a number of different forms. Community organizations of all types, including church groups, can be mobilized. Informal pressures upon real estate operators and mortgagers can be effective. The private, if not public, support of Negro leaders for controlled migration can be achieved. At Concord Park and Greenbelt Knoll, the builders found no opposition from Negroes to a balanced community pattern, once it was explained that the larger goal was to break down racial segregation. Many Negroes will support policies aimed at avoiding all-Negro communities if alternative housing opportunities are available.

The moral problem is not an easy one. It is the problem of placing limits upon Negro in-migration to particular urban and suburban areas. It means fostering a smaller discrimination in favor of scotching a larger one. Whatever the difficulties of such a position, it seems to be, for a large number of Negroes and whites alike, a preferable alternative to the present pattern of segregated population groups.

Returning White Population to Central Cities

Values of urbanism, other things being equal, compete easily with the suburban way of life. The other things now *not* equal include: modern, moderate priced housing; cleanliness and green space; good schools; safety against hoodlum attack; a sense of neighborhood solidarity. If such amenities were available, the attractions of urban life would almost certainly be sufficient to bring large numbers of white residents back into the cities. The cities offer a diversity of living conditions, a choice of companionship, and a range of leisure time activities that cannot be matched by the suburbs with their relatively closed and static conditions of life. The isolation of the dormitory suburbs, the large fraction of life demanded for commuting, and the social restriction of village living have already produced a swelling protest. Some segment of the metropolitan population is certainly composed of confirmed suburbanites, and no changes in the central city would attract them. But urban life would beckon large numbers if it could compete with suburbia in terms of the economics of housing, the safety and comfort of families, and the social solidarity of neighborhoods.

No precise data exist concerning the extent to which the suburban sadness has already started a return flow to the cities. Certainly that flow has been considerable, especially among older couples, the more wealthy, and the childless. (The Chicago Gold Coast and the Manhattan luxury apartments would make important foci of research for measuring this flow.) What needs to be done is to bring into this stream the larger numbers of young and middle-aged couples who have families and who are not wealthy. Developments within the suburbs—the overcrowding of schools, the blighting of badly planned residential areas, and the full flowering of the uninhibited automobile culture—will provide an additional push toward the cities.

Whatever may be accomplished by individual home owners and real estate specialists will not be sufficient to reverse the massive population trends described earlier. The effort must be aided by governmental action. The important point is that governmental programs must be on a far larger scale than any action thus far undertaken.

The basic unit of operation must be a large site: a complete neighborhood or even a complete area of the city. The scale of urban renewal must be conceived not in square blocks, but in square miles. Destruction or rehabilitation of old urban dwellings and the building of new neighborhoods must be planned not in tens of acres but in hundreds. Whole sections of cities will have to be made over in order to attract an influx of stable white population groups.

Rebuilding on this scale is important for many reasons. And it would provide one opportunity to achieve interracial communities. Many white families affirm that they move to the suburbs not because they have Negroes for neighbors but because of the neighborhood deterioration that accompanies the high densities and rowdy behavior of the in-migrants. Large rebuilt areas, strictly controlled against over-crowding, would have the effect of removing such objections. Very large sums of public money will be required for this sort of program, but the obstacles are political rather than economic.[10] Intricate collaborative devices among the local, state, and federal governments will be necessary. The history of urban redevelopment thus far, with few exceptions, is a history of too little, too late. Anything less than a massive program may have admirable local effects for particular population fractions, as when adequate housing is substituted for slum housing over several blocks for a few residents in New York's Harlem. These ameliorative programs are not to be criticized. But they do not attack the basic problem of the bifurcation of races on urban-suburban lines. To meet this problem, the rebuilding of entire sections of major cities is necessary.

The Suburbanization of Negroes

Any extensive rebuilding of central cities will displace Negro populations who inhabit the very urban areas most in need of rebuilding. No progress is possible unless a redistribution of the Negro population simultaneously occurs. One objective must be a migration of Negroes to suburban areas.

It is widely assumed that opening suburbs to Negroes would be readily achieved if there existed a single local government whose jurisdiction covered the entire metropolitan area. This is certainly too optimistic a view of the matter. Even under a metropolitan government, the people in outlying areas would not be without ability to resist, politically and socially, the incursion of what they consider "undesirable elements" into their communities. In Chicago and in many other places, residents of "better" neighborhoods *within* the central city have successfully opposed housing measures which threatened to bring Negro residents into their areas. If the free distribution of nonwhite groups is not politically feasible on an interneighborhood basis, the creation of a metropolitan government will certainly not make it so on an intercity one. A single government for a whole area might conceivably provide a more satisfactory political arena for the eventual solution of distributing nonwhite groups throughout an entire metropolitan area, but will not *ipso facto* guarantee that distribution.

Nor is it true that restrictions on the migration of Negro and other nonwhite groups to the suburbs is solely a class or economic matter. Any examination of the variety of suburban conditions leads to the conclusion that urban blight and the dilapidated housing and social conditions that accompany it are not uniquely characteristic of the central cities. Rather, blight exists in varying degrees of intensity in all parts of the metropolitan area, central city and suburbs alike. In all but the very newest of planned suburban developments, many dwelling units exist which, in the terms of the Bureau of the Census, "should be torn down, extensively repaired, or rebuilt." Only a fraction of these units are Negro dwellings. In many metropolitan areas a larger proportion of dwelling units outside than inside the central city are dilapidated or lack running water.[11]

Despite these facts, in many suburban areas the extravagances of legal restrictions covering suburban building should be examined for their effect upon maintaining Negro urban concentrations. Provisions covering lot sizes, sidewalks, streets, building setbacks, and building materials often have very little to do with the maintenance of standards of health and decency. They are, rather, frankly established to stabilize or to upgrade community levels, including the maintenance of their racial character. The effect is to make suburban housing too expensive for even the Negroes who otherwise could afford, and would prefer, suburban living. Less extravagant building and housing codes would certainly lead to some greater degree of Negro suburbanization. This can be accomplished without producing additional suburban slums. The antidote to over-stringent building restrictions is not their complete abolition.

Nondiscriminatory housing laws would, as we have seen, go a long way in encouraging some suburbanization of Negroes. Other discriminating practices—many of them extra-legal—should be ended. If local building inspectors cannot be trained to administer laws impartially, they should be replaced by officials who can, under state or federal supervision. If local police forces will not protect the property and lives of Negro purchasers of suburban homes, then procedures for training, replacing, or penalizing such officials must be adopted. If established realtors will not sell to Negroes, others should be encouraged, and perhaps paid, to do so.

Social attitudes change more slowly than laws, and only a moderate incursion of Negroes into established suburbs can be expected in the near future. The best chance for even this modest development is under community auspices on the basis of controlled migrations. The need for Negro suburban housing will greatly exceed the receptivity of the established suburbs, especially if central city rebuilding is undertaken on the scale that it is needed. This sharply raises the question of the desirability of encouraging all-Negro suburbs.

The negative consideration is obvious: all-Negro suburbs would simply substitute one sort of segregated life for another. On the other hand, there is much to be said on the positive side. Such suburbs would be a large factor in redressing the present imbalance in the urban-suburban population distribution. As we have seen, this in itself is a highly desirable step. Secondly, such communities, adequately planned and constructed, would provide a great improvement in living conditions, superior to both the urban and suburban slums in which so large a proportion of Negroes now reside. Thirdly, and perhaps most importantly, the all-Negro middle-class suburb could very well constitute a significant step in the direction of large-scale interracial communities. Present conditions of life of the largest fraction of the Negro population discourage, rather than encourage, the habits of thought and conduct deemed desirable by the larger white community. The middle-class Negro suburb would foster such attributes. If class, in addition to skin color, is a principal cause of segregation, then the class differential may be overcome by the middle-class suburban life.

As in so many planned social changes, schemes for all-Negro suburban communities may produce unexpected ill consequences. One deserves mention. Grant the truth of what has been said: that good suburban housing in a good suburban neighborhood will aid in producing a Negro population of model, middle-class, social attributes, and that nothing distinguishes this group from middle-class whites except skin color. It is then easily assumed that interracial living is the next step. But the opposite assumption must also be entertained: that whites will continue to resist interracial living. In this event Negroes will all the more resent their segregation and whites will have no line except the color line on which to take a stand. If Negro-white tensions pivot exclusively on color, they may be exacerbated to a new point of bitterness.

Despite such dangers, the more persuasive evidence is that Negro-white tensions will decrease, not increase, as the populations become socially more alike. For this reason, as well as the need to meet short-run housing requirements, experiments with all-Negro suburban communities should be encouraged.

Negroes to Smaller Cities

Discussion of the possible distribution of some Negroes to points outside the larger metropolitan areas does not fall strictly within the purposes of this paper. Yet it is worth noting that Negroes are greatly underrepresented in virtually all places outside the South and the larger urban areas of the rest of the country. Without considering nonsouthern rural areas (where Negroes constitute a smaller fraction of the population than anywhere else), the cities under 250 thousand in the Northeast are, in all size classes, less than 2.9 per cent Negro; in the North Central states, less than 4.2 per cent; and in the West, less than 2.7 per cent.[12] A program of encouraging migration to these smaller cities would somewhat mitigate the large city, urban-suburban racial bifurcation and, at the same time, establish important new opportunities for integrated living. The effects of such an effort should not be overestimated. For example, if one unrealistically assumes it were possible for nonsouthern cities of from 10 thousand to 250 thousand population to be increased 5 per cent in total population by an in-migration of Negroes, the total number so placed would be fewer than 900 thousand. This is only some 150 thousand more than the number of Negroes in New York City at the 1950 census.

Nevertheless, attempts to locate Negroes in cities of this size —as well as in smaller urban areas—would be worthwhile. Since employment opportunities in industry constitute the most important attraction for Negro in-migrants, success of such attempts would pivot upon the availability of such jobs for Negroes (therefore a shortage of white workers) and upon information concerning such opportunities being disseminated among potential migrants. The former factor will to a large extent depend upon further industrial growth in small- and medium-size urban areas. The factor of publicity is more immediately controllable. The information flow now directed at potential migrants from the South (by such organizations as the Urban League) could very well be focused more sharply on the existing and emerging opportunities outside the larger metropolitan areas.

No single measure will solve the problem in any single area, and the same combination of measures will not be appropriate as leverage points in any two areas. What strikes the observer is the paucity of imagination that has been brought to bear on the issue. The Quaker communities in the Philadelphia area provide a model for one kind of controlled migration that is only slowly being taken up in other places. The investment in almost any city of, say, a million dollars in a revolving fund for the purchase of homes to foster interracial neighborhoods, with careful planning and public relations, could make a dent in the pattern of segregation. A well-staffed, resourceful office with the objective of publicizing successes of interracial residential contacts would be a valuable positive aid to enlarging those contacts and no less valuable a means of dissipating images of disagreeableness and violence that widely prevail.

Action programs of this sort are obvious needs. Beyond them there exists a wide range of more experimental possibilities for both private and public agencies. For example, there are a number of newly built areas in the central cities whose attractiveness and proximity to work and recreational facilities make them highly desirable living places. Lake Meadows, in Chicago, is a good example of this sort of development. Nevertheless, these areas tend to become all-Negro communities because of their relatively small size, or their situation close to older Negro slums, or other factors. It might be possible to make such newly built areas model interracial neighborhoods. How can white residents be attracted to them? A private foundation might bring the attractions of such developments to the attention of whites by maintaining a good small museum at such a site or by arranging concerts there (but at no other nearby place) of outstanding musical groups, or by providing superior park and swimming facilities, or indeed by partially subsidizing rental costs for limited periods. The marginal attractions needed to bring whites into such intrinsically attractive areas may in many cases be quite small; and once a pattern of interracial living is successfully achieved it may be expected to continue as subsidies are diminished. Private organizations could in a similar way reward suburban communities that make it easy for Negroes to take up residence.

The national government may not be barred from an analogous type of activity. A good case can be made for a federal program to provide suburbs with aid for community facilities they already need and will need even more in years to come: schools, parks, libraries, swimming pools, and similar amenities. It is commonplace for federal legislation to establish conditions that must be met by local governments before they qualify for financial aid. The question arises: is it possible to write a federal law that would supply aid for community facilities on a priority basis to those suburbs containing a given minimum of Negro residents? Constitutional and political questions immediately arise. Clearly no requirement based directly upon a racial classification would meet constitutional standards. Yet it is not beyond the realm of legal creativity to find another scheme of definition that would foster the end of racial distribution and yet remain with constitutional limits. The more difficult objection is political, but it is by no means insurmountable. Even southern congressmen might support such a measure if for no other reason than glee over the embarrassment of their northern colleagues. The larger point is not to argue for the desirability or feasibility of this particular measure, but rather to suggest the need for inventive action. The growing consequences of the population schism, plus the plight that many suburbs will soon find themselves in, combine to bring within the realm of probability even schemes that at first blush seem impossible of achievement.

The whole discussion of "solutions" now rests too largely upon moral terms. The wealth of the United States has historically been used to remove issues from the idealistic to a cash basis, and in this issue, too, cash may be a great salve for moral wounds. This is not meant to be a cynical statement. It is, rather, counsel for the strategy of induced social change. Payment in the form of needed community facilities should accompany other types of action.

Church, social work, and educational institutions must prepare the ground for interracial living and must be ready to act when tensions occur. Indeed, mobilization of resources must take place over a very wide range: from training police officers in problems of race relations to the establishment of special community programs for the improvement of interracial contacts; from the provision of social services for Negro in-migrants to education programs for prospective employers of Negroes; from block activity preparing the way for Negro neighbors to nationwide programs that implement basic Negro civil rights. Every community facility—churches, schools, labor unions, recreational groups, economic organizations, and government—can be enlisted. Here, as with almost all programs of civic change, working through established institutions and existing voluntary groups is the best avenue to success.

Conclusion

It is frequently argued that problems created by the present distribution of Negroes in the large metropolitan areas are only transitory problems. They will solve themselves through the normal processes of acculturation. This view holds that every immigrant wave to the great cities has at least initially produced disadvantaged ethnic islands. With the passage of time, however, these islands have given way as the second and third generations have acquired cultural characteristics of the larger society and broken away from the habits of conduct of their immigrant fathers and grandfathers. This is the pattern of the Jews in New York, the Poles in Chicago, the Italians in San Francisco. There is some evidence that the Negro group is going through the same process as its members surmount social, vocational, professional, and residential barriers. All the problem needs is time. The American melting pot will work for Negroes as it has for others.

This is a hopeful view. Despite any examples of successful interracial adjustment, it is a view not substantiated by either history or available data. The example of earlier European immigrants all concern white populations. No statistically significant evidence exists indicating the inevitable dissolution of the Negro concentrations. As with Japanese-Americans before World War II, acceptance by the larger community for a relatively few Negroes is being accompanied by life within closed communities for the relatively many. (The Japanese community in Los Angeles grew continuously between 1900 and 1942.) The factor of skin color, alone, is one cause for the different course of development. The very size of the Negro concentration in the larger cities, resulting in the establishment of an entire Negro economic and social life, can also be expected to obstruct the decline of the communities in which that life flourishes. To this must be added the disinclination of many white groups to accept Negroes as neighbors and social companions. The total picture for the future, if present trends are unaltered, is the further breaking down of some boundaries of the closed community affecting proportionately small numbers of Negroes. For the largest numbers, segregation will continue and probably increase, rather than decline.

This is almost certainly the correct prognosis for the immediate 30 years ahead. To the extent that the natural acculturation argument is one covering the distant future—say 80 or 100 years —it may have greater accuracy. But to that extent it is largely irrelevant. The central cities of the metropolitan areas dominate the nation not only in population but also in retail and wholesale sales, manufacturing, and the provision of services to individuals and businesses. They set the tone and pattern for the entire complex of community interdependence in politics, economics, and cultural life. If the analysis presented here is accurate, the whole nation is faced with a wide range of deleterious consequences. And these consequences will take their toll long before the "natural desuetude" of segregation is accomplished. This is the justification for taking all positive steps possible to end the present patterns of segregation.

Another reason for not distrubing the current population distribution might lie in the danger that dispersion would deprive Negroes of the political power they have acquired as the consequence of concentration. This is not a valid argument for two reasons.

On the one hand, it does not take into account the genuine gains that accrue to the Negro population as the consequence of dispersion. Increasing strain in race relations seems always to accompany concentrated numbers. Where a minority group is dispersed, it is less visible, less likely to be considered a unit, less feared, less subject to discrimination. Where it is concentrated and segregated, it is more likely to be relegated to a subordinate position, and its members have fewer opportunities for assimilation into the larger social structure.

On the other hand, dispersion of residential areas would not necessarily lead to a decline in Negro political power. The 100 per cent Negro voting districts can be viewed as a type of gerrymandering in which political power is lost by the very concentration of voters. Negroes constituting 50 percent of the voters in two election districts (or 25 per cent in four districts) will wield more political power than if they composed 100 per cent of a single district. What is to be avoided is the halfway house: not enough dispersion to prevent clear subordination, with not enough concentration to make numbers politically effective. Within the larger metropolitan areas this is an unlikely possibility. The gains to be made by Negroes from political action built upon concentration can never equal those that can be achieved by dispersion throughout the metropolitan areas.

The programs suggested for overcoming Negro concentrations face great obstacles. They arouse the ire of the ignorant and the prejudiced. They are disquieting to even the fair-minded and the sophisticated who live good lives and who perform their civic duties conscientiously. And they will be bitterly opposed by a wide range of people: owners, mortgagers, and others who profit from the present patterns of land use; political leaders in the central cities, including Negro leaders, who fear the dissipation of established constituencies, as well as political leaders of other areas whose tenure will be disturbed by the incursion of new voters into their districts; old residents of suburbs and the better central-city neighborhoods who hold strongly to their comfortable social situations and established shopping, social, and educational patterns. Even those with humanitarian motives will voice opposition to some plans on the grounds that they constitute an unwarranted interference in the life patterns of the poor. And Negro groups and leaders will not easily be won over to some aspects of the proposed program. They will, for example, see large-scale urban renewal as a displacement and an imposition, before its advantages will be apparent. Negroes have already in many cities distinguished themselves for their opposition to smaller-scale programs of urban renewal.[13] Some of this opposition may be blunted: as when Negro opposition to urban renewal is placated by well-planned programs of relocation housing. But every such move, in turn, is likely to increase opposition from other sources: in the example given from areas in which the relocation housing is to be placed.

Despite difficulties and despite the uncertainty of success, all efforts are justified. The stakes are high: the preservation and further development of many facets of urban American life, for whites and Negroes alike. By building a nondiscriminatory housing market in both city and suburbs, income and social attributes, not race, can be maximized as the criteria for residential location. By rebuilding large areas of central cities, white populations can be induced to return to those cities. By combating restrictions against Negro occupancy of suburbs, a flow of nonwhites can be started in that direction. By attracting Negroes to jobs in the smaller cities outside the South, where they are now underrepresented, some of the present and potential city-suburban population imbalance may be corrected. By encouraging through community resources the controlled migration of Negroes into all areas of city and suburbs, a significant redistribution of Negroes and whites can take place. All these measures minimize the dangerous operation of the tip-point psychology. Here, as elsewhere, nothing succeeds like success, and a demonstration that such a program can produce results in one metropolitan area of the nation will be important for all areas. The only way to avoid the consequences of racial schism is to bridge it.[14]

NOTES

1. Otis D. Duncan and Beverly Duncan, *The Negro Population of Chicago* (Chicago: University of Chicago Press, 1957), p. 96.
2. *Ibid.*, p. 120.
3. With respect to the latter point see Robert C. Weaver, "Integration in Public and Private Housing," *Annals of the American Academy of Political and Social Science,* March, 1956, p. 87.
4. Otis D. Duncan and Beverly Duncan, *op. cit.*, pp. 14–16, chaps. vii, viii.
5. See, for example, Davis McEntire, "A Study of Racial Attitudes in Neighborhoods Infiltrated by Non-Whites" (mimeographed) (Berkeley: University of California, 1955); Arnold M. Rose, Frank J. Atelsek, and Lawrence R. McDonald, "Neighborhood Reactions to Isolated Negro Residents: An Alternative to Invasion and Succession," *American Sociological Review,* October, 1953, pp. 497–507; Robert C. Weaver, "Integration in Public and Private Housing," *loc. cit.;* also the mimeographed reports of the Committee on Civil Rights in Manhattan, "Open Occupancy Living in the Bronx" (May, 1957); "Summary of Survey on Country-Wide Instances of Open Occupancy Housing" (May, 1957).
6. Quoted from Edward C. Banfield and Morton Grodzins, *Government and Housing in Metropolitan Areas* (New York: McGraw-Hill Book Co., 1958).
7. See Shirley A. Star, "Interracial Tension in Two Areas of Chicago: An Exploratory Approach to the Measurement of Interracial Tension," unpublished doctoral dissertation, Department of Sociology, University of Chicago, December, 1950.
8. Evelyn M. Kitagawa and Donald J. Bogue, *Suburbanization of Manufacturing Activity Within Standard Metropolitan Areas* (Published jointly by Scripps Foundation for Research in Population Problems, Miami University, and Population Research and Training Center, University of Chicago), 1955, p. 15.
9. See Robert C. Weaver, "The Effect of Anti-Discrimination Legislation Upon the FHA- and VA-Insured Housing Market in New York State," *Land Economics,* Vol. XXXI, No. 4 (November, 1955), pp. 303–13.
10. See Edward C. Banfield and Morton Grodzins, *op. cit.*

11. Victor Jones, "Local Government Organization in Metropolitan Area," in Coleman Woodbury (ed.), *The Future of Cities and Urban Redevelopment* (Chicago: University of Chicago Press, 1953).
12. Otis D. Duncan and Albert J. Reiss, Jr., *Social Characteristics of Urban and Rural Communities, 1950* (New York: John Wiley & Sons, 1956), p. 60.
13. For good reasons, it should be added. Renewal programs are largely slum clearance programs and, therefore, largely affect Negro populations. Since alternative housing is frequently unavailable, the effect of slum clearance is often one of packing Negroes even tighter into existing Negro areas, usually in the periphery of the cleared zone. A study by the Urban League of Chicago showed that between 1948 and 1956, 86,000 people in Chicago were displaced by urban renewal, highway, and other programs. Almost 57,000 of these were Negroes. Constituting fewer than 20 per cent of the city's population, Negroes made up more than 65 per cent of the displaced population. See *Chicago Urban League Newsletter,* Vol 2, No. 4 (September-October, 1957), pp. 3–4.
14. Earlier versions of portions of these materials have been published as "Metropolitan Segregation," *Scientific American,* Vol. 197 (October, 1957), pp. 33–41; and "The New Shame of the Cities," *Confluence,* Vol. 7, No. 1 (Spring, 1958), pp. 29–46.

8 *The Apocalyptic Future*

Despite their awareness that disorder, decay and disintegration may lie ahead, most sociologists implicitly take an optimistic view of the future. Hopeful that knowledge may make it possible to avoid catastrophe, they often fail to spell out the dire eventualities that might come to pass. Rejecting any form of determinism, they self-consciously eschew the role of Cassandra, however menacing the omens. It therefore falls to others to make explicit the unwanted and even unthinkable historical possibilities. The following brief selections from nonacademic sources provide an apocalyptic vision of what may happen if present trends continue and nothing is done to deal with the problems so clearly evident in American cities.

The Urban Fortress

NATIONAL COMMISSION ON THE CAUSES AND PREVENTION OF VIOLENCE

Drawn from the Commission's report on violent crime, this excerpt offers a description of what urban America might become if the problem of public order is not dealt with at its source, that is, in the social conditions now present or emerging in our central cities.

In the absence of the massive action that seems to be needed to overcome this deficit [of unsatisfied needs and aspirations], our cities are being misshaped in other ways by actions of more affluent citizens who desire safety for themselves, their families, and their investments. The safety they are getting is not the safety without fear that comes from ameliorating the causes of violent crime; rather it is the precarious safety obtained through individual efforts at self-defense. Thus the way in which we have so far chosen to deal with the deepening problem of violent crime begins to revise the future shape of our cities. In a few more years, lacking effective public action, this is how these cities will likely look:

Central business districts in the heart of the city, surrounded by mixed areas of accelerating deterioration, will be partially protected by large numbers of people shopping or working in commercial buildings during daytime hours, plus a substantial police presence, and will be largely deserted except for police patrols during nighttime hours.

High-rise apartment buildings and residential compounds protected by private guards and security devices will be fortified cells for upper-middle and high-income populations living at prime locations in the city.

Suburban neighborhoods, geographically far removed from the central city, will be protected mainly by economic homogeneity and by distance from population groups with the highest propensities to commit crimes.

Lacking a sharp change in federal and state policies, ownership of guns will be almost universal in the suburbs, homes will be fortified by an array of devices from window grills to electronic surveillance equipment, armed citizen volunteers in cars will supplement inadequate police patrols in neighborhoods closer to the central city, and extreme left-wing and right-wing groups will have tremendous armories of weapons which could be brought into play with or without provocation.

High-speed, patrolled expressways will be sanitized corridors connecting safe areas, and private automobiles, taxicabs, and commercial vehicles will be routinely equipped with unbreakable glass, light armor, and other security features. Inside garages or valet parking will be available at safe buildings in or near the central city. Armed guards will "ride shotgun" on all forms of public transportation.

Streets and residential neighborhoods in the central city will be unsafe in differing degrees, and the ghetto slum neighborhoods will be places of terror with widespread crime, perhaps entirely out of police control during nighttime hours. Armed guards will protect all public facilities such as schools, libraries, and playgrounds in these areas.

Between the unsafe, deteriorating central city on the one hand and the network of safe, prosperous areas and sanitized corridors on the other, there will be, not unnaturally, intensifying hatred and deepening division. Violence will increase further, and the defensive response of the affluent will become still more elaborate.

Inevitability Comes to New York

RUSSELL BAKER

This selection by Russell Baker, a regular columnist for The New York Times, *was provoked by the massive electrical blackout that hit the entire east coast of the United States in 1965. Despite its tongue-in-cheek quality, it demonstrates clearly the extent to which modern urban life rests upon a complex and interdependent technological system—and what might happen if that structure were suddenly to collapse.*

The end came on Sept. 17, 1973. It had been forecast by an M.I.T. undergraduate who had been running the law of probability through his computer.

The frequency of malfunction in New York, his computer noted, had increased at such a rate than an ultimate day of total breakdown was a statistical certainty by the early 1970's. Naturally, no one took the forecast as anything more than an undergraduate hoax.

The chain of events on that last day began at Shea Stadium at 4:43 P.M. when the Mets finished a scoreless ninth inning against the Mexico City Braves, thus becoming the first team in history to lose 155 games in a single baseball season.

Two minutes later, Irma Arnstadt, a Bronx housewife, turned on the kitchen faucet and noticed that there was no water. Going to her telephone, she dialed her plumber, not knowing that at that very moment, in defiance of the law of probability, 6,732,548 other persons in New York were simultaneously dialing telephone numbers.

Mrs. Arnstadt's call was the one that broke the system's back. Somewhere in a sealed windowless building a transistor gasped and failed. Under the incredible overload, other transistors all over the city groaned and gave up.

And so, with the telephones out, it was hours before the authorities could learn that there was not a drop of water left anywhere in the pipes of the five boroughs.

The press might have detected it almost immediately, but, as chance would have it, the biennial newspaper strike began that day at 5 P.M. and not a single newspaperman was on duty.

At 5:03 P.M., outside the Waldorf-Astoria Hotel, a taxi driver was shot by a man who had been trying unsuccessfully for fifty-five minutes to get a cab. It was later established that the man had been trying futilely to find an empty cab during the rush hour in Manhattan for sixteen years. "I just snapped," he said later. "That was a day when everything seemed to just snap."

News of the shooting spread rapidly through the city's cab fleet. Panic seized the drivers who feared a general uprising by the rush-hour hordes signaling vainly for taxicabs. As a result the drivers abandoned their hacks in the streets.

By 5:30 P.M. the resulting traffic jam extended from Trenton to New Haven. Two minutes later, a radio sports reporter announced that the Yankees had dropped their fourth in a row to the Milwaukee Athletics and were, thus, once again mathematically eliminated from any possibility of finishing in the first division.

This news was interrupted by a bulletin reporting that more than fifty knifings had occurred simultaneously on fifty different subway trains scattered throughout the city and that the subway trainmen had walked out on a wildcat strike to press demands for more police protection.

At City Hall, there was no hint that anything untoward was happening until 5:12 P.M. when it began to snow. The Mayor watched the snow for perhaps twenty minutes and then summoned his press adviser. "What is that?" he asked, pointing out the window. "Snow, your honor," said the press adviser, who was one of the brighter products of the Democratic machine that had been returned to power after John Lindsay had gone on to more manageable tasks than governing New York.

The Mayor was aggrieved. "In the old days, when the machine was running this city right," said the Mayor, "it never snowed in September." "True, said the press adviser, "but the machine is like everything else in New York these days. It doesn't work."

All over the city, with no water left in the pipes, no subways running, no telephone service, no newspapers, the snow pouring down and both the Mets and the Yankees dead, people felt in a gay festive mood. And so, as people will under hardship, millions decided to spend a night on the town.

In the theater district alone, 500,000 people appeared at box offices demanding theater tickets, which then retailed at $79.90 per seat. With vast lines at every box office, the manager of a theater in 43rd Street announced at 8:22 P.M. that there were no tickets available for anybody without enough influence to rate a good table at Twenty-One.

New Yorkers, being New Yorkers, might not have broken even then, except for a Brooklyn man named Omar. At that moment in Brooklyn, Omar plugged in his electric carving knife and the entire Atlantic seaboard from Labrador to Chattanooga was plunged into blackness.

By next morning, of course—we all know the story—volunteers began bringing out the first New York survivors, and six days later the President viewed the area in a flying inspection tour and ordered his historic reevaluation of American civilization.

Which, as everybody knows, is why nobody lives in cities any more.

For Further Reading

Banfield, Edward C. *The Unheavenly City*. Boston: Little, Brown, 1970.

A controversial book that argues that most urban problems stem from an unassimilated lower class and that these problems are more likely to be resolved by "anonymous" social, economic, and political forces than by well-intentioned efforts to "do something."

Downs, Anthony. *Urban Problems and Prospects*. Chicago: Markham, 1970.

Essays by a perceptive analyst on the institutional changes that might be necessary in order to deal with urban problems.

Greer, Scott. *The Emerging Metropolis*. New York: Free Press of Glencoe, 1962.

A leading urban sociologist offers an analysis that focusses upon the causes and consequences of the increasing scale of urban society.

Gruen, Victor. *The Heart of Our Cities.* New York: Simon and Schuster, 1964.

A noted architect who is committed to the idea that the central city can—and should—be maintained or restored offers a diagnosis of present difficulties and proposes measures to solve them.

Gutkind, Erwin A. *The Twilight of Cities.* New York: Free Press of Glencoe, 1962.

A wide-ranging historical and comparative account that foresees the disappearance of cities as we have known them and the emergence of new forms of community within a regional structure.

Mumford, Lewis. *The Urban Prospect.* New York: Harcourt Brace Jovanovich, 1968.

Essays by a distinguished historian and philosopher of city life whose ideas, though often challenging and controversial, are invariably stimulating and often wise and penetrating.

Rodwin, Lloyd (ed.). *The Future Metropolis.* New York: Braziller, 1961.

Essays by a number of authorities who explore present problems and the factors that are likely to shape the cities of the future.

Warner, Sam Bass (ed.). *Planning for a Nation of Cities.* Cambridge, Mass.: M.I.T. Press, 1966.

A useful collection of papers dealing with urban problems, the possibilities of planning, and the role of government in shaping the character of cities.

Index